THE FURROW BEHIND ME

THE FURROW
BEHIND ME

The Autobiography of a Hebridean Crofter

TOLD BY

Angus MacLellan

TRANSLATED BY

John Lorne Campbell

Birlinn

This edition published in 1997 by
Birlinn Limited
Unit 8
Canongate Venture
5 New Street
Edinburgh EH8 8BH

British Library Cataloguing-in-Publication Data
A Catalogue record of this book is available from the British Library

ISBN 1 874744 27 0

Printed and bound in Finland by Werner Söderström OY

For M.F.S.C.

CONTENTS

	INTRODUCTION	*page* xi
	CHRONOLOGY	xix
1	BOYHOOD ON SOUTH UIST	1
2	THE MILITIA	16
3	TIRINIE	25
4	BORENICH	60
5	ROWARDENNAN	77
6	DALMALLY	156
7	SOUTH UIST AGAIN	177
	NOTES	195
	GLOSSARY OF AGRICULTURAL TERMS	201

Dr John Lorne Campbell (1906–96), scholar and farmer, dedicated his career to the recording, transmission and publication of the Gaelic song, literary and linguistic record of Scotland. His meeting with Angus MacLellan in Lochboisdale in the winter of 1948–9 led to the recording of Angus' personal reminiscences as well as of his huge stock of stories and ballads. The original Gaelic biography was subsequently published as *Saoghal an Treobhaiche* in Norway (1965) and in Scotland (1972). This had instigated a lengthy and successful phase of recording song and story in South Uist in the 1950s and 1960s and set the seal on Dr Campbell's pioneering collecting work which had begun in Barra in the early 1930s.

From his boyhood at Inverneill and Taynish on the mainland of Argyll, John Lorne Campbell went to St John's College, Oxford, where he studied agriculture with Professor Sir James Scott Watson, graduating in 1929. He had learnt some Gaelic from a Tiree man, Hector MacLean, Ground Officer of the Taynish Estate, and at Oxford he began, in his spare time, the serious study of the language with Professor John Fraser. While at Oxford, he also began work on an anthology of Gaelic songs of the Jacobite Rising of 1745–6, which was published as *Highland Songs of the '45* in 1933 and republished in a second edition by the Scottish Gaelic Texts Society in 1983. In August 1933, John Lorne Campbell went to Barra to study crofting conditions and colloquial Gaelic. There he found a 'community of independent personalities where memories of men and events are often amazingly long; in the Gaelic-speaking Hebrides they go back to Viking times a thousand years ago.' His mentor was John Macpherson, 'the Coddy', whose lore has been preserved in *Tales of Barra* (1960). With Compton Mackenzie, then living in Barra, Campbell vigorously entered the economic and political life of the Hebrides by founding the Sea League, campaigning for the enforcement of fishing limits and the closure of the Minch to trawlers to protect the livelihood of the Islands.

In his approach to Celtic Studies, he recognised the importance of grasping a good dialect thoroughly and of learning the language from the inside. 'Book Gaelic' could be an obstacle to learning since, in his own words, 'all spoken Gaelic dialects differ from the literary language, in some respects consistently: the dialects of the Outer Hebrides are in fact more vigorous than the modern literary language, and contain many words and expressions that are not in the printed dictionaries.' He pioneered the use of mechanical and electrical recording equipment and took it acrosss the Atlantic in 1937 to record the descendants of Barra and

South Uist emigrants in Nova Scotia. Source of the results of these efforts have been published in *Sia Sgialachdan* (1939), the three volumes of *Hebridean Folksongs* (1969–81) and *Songs Remembered in Exile* (1990). Other topics developed by John Lorne have been the researches of the Celtic Scholar, Edward Lhuyd, the poetry and song of Alasdair MacMhaighstir Alasdair, and the incomparable folklore collections of Fr Allan McDonald, parish priest of Daliburgh and Eriskay. This original and outstanding work brought John Lorne Campbell honorary degrees from St Francis Xavier University, Nova Scotia, and Glasgow University, and a D.Litt. for his published research from Oxford.

In 1938 Dr Campbell bought the islands of Canna and Sanday and farmed them in the traditional manner until 1981 when he presented them to the National Trust for Scotland. In 1935 he had married Margaret Fay Shaw, an American who was collecting Gaelic song in South Uist and this longstanding partnership brought together her musical talents with his language skills to create a unique store in Canna and a lasting monument to their dedicated scholarship.

HUGH CHEAPE
National Museums of Scotland

INTRODUCTION

THIS IS a unique autobiography. It was tape-recorded between January 1960 and April 1961 from Angus McLellan, the well-known Gaelic storyteller[1] who is now living in retirement at Frobost in the island of South Uist in the Outer Hebrides, and is now translated from the Gaelic, which has been transcribed, the first autobiography of its kind in the Scottish Gaelic language.[2]

Angus MacLellan was born on the 4th July 1869 at Poll Torain, Loch Eynort, South Uist, and was baptized by Fr MacColl at Bornish nine days later. He was the youngest son in a family of four brothers and four sisters, two of whom, besides Angus, are still living. Their father was Angus Mac-Lellan, and their mother's maiden name was Catherine Wilson; she came from Benbecula. Angus's father was a land-less cottar, but the MacLellans had always lived around Loch Eynort and Benmore in South Uist, and had seen better days before the crofters on the east coast of Uist had been dispossessed of their land and their hill grazings had been given to big sheep farmers.[3]

Loch Eynort is a long, narrow, winding arm of the sea running far inland into the island of South Uist between the hills that lie on the east side of the island. In olden days it was the main harbour of South Uist, but its difficult entrance and strong tidal currents were always a disadvantage, and latterly it was superseded by Lochboisdale for this purpose. Angus's parents' thatched house still stands on the south side of the loch, facing north-east. West of the head of Loch Eynort lies the flat part of South Uist, consisting of grassy pasture and innumerable lochs, while along the Atlantic shore of the island lies a flat sandy plain broken only by sand-hills, known as the 'machair'. There are thus two entirely different types of soil in Uist, calcareous sand in the west and acid peat in the east, and in the old days, at any rate, the west bred landsmen and the east bred fishermen, and the latter were the more independent of the two.

Poverty was widespread amongst the Gaelic-speaking crofters and cottars of South Uist during the first half of Angus MacLellan's life. The Jacobite defeat at Culloden in 1746 had led to the immediate suppression of local liberties and ultimately to the ending of the paternalistic proprietorship of the old Clanranald family, who had been staunch Jacobites, Catholics, and patrons of Gaelic literature (the last court poetry written in classical Gaelic was produced on South Uist, by the MacVurichs). The last Clanranald of the old line was an absentee, and during his time the people of Uist were abandoned to the principles of *laissez faire*. During the first two decades of the nineteenth century, large profits were made by Highland proprietors from the manufacture of kelp from seaweed. So an attempt was made to rationalize the economy of many Highland estates by depriving the small tenants of their traditional hill grazings and giving these to big sheep farmers, while the small tenants themselves were shifted to poorer holdings near the shore to make kelp for the lairds. When the price of kelp dropped after the removal of the duty on barilla in the 1820s the bottom fell out of this system, and the poorer part of the population had to bear the brunt. This left the Highlands and Islands, and nowhere more than South Uist, with contrasts of wealth and poverty comparable to what now exists in Southern Italy, and a bitter land question which was to bedevil Highland politics for three generations. In South Uist this was intensified by differences in religion between the estate management and the large farmers (who came from outside) on the one hand, and the indigeneous crofters and cottars on the other.

In the nineteenth century, the Gaelic-speaking population of the Highlands and Islands had none of the linguistic rights now usually claimed by minorities. Hence a man or woman who did not know English was liable to be taken advantage of in various ways. In some parts of the Highlands there was a tradition of bilingualism, but not in the Isles, where Gaelic was the universal language and the cultivation of its tremendous and beautiful oral tradition was at the one time the main form of social entertainment and an escape from the harsh realities of present existence. Before the Crofters' Act of 1886, granting security of tenure and fair rents, the crofters held what land they had on the estate's own terms, they worked for the big farmers on the big farmers' own terms, and they bartered most of their produce with the merchants on the merchants' own terms. It was worse for the cottars who, holding no land of their own, could only get permission to cultivate or graze someone else's at an exhorbitant price, as happened to Angus's father. Medical service was completely inadequate; the dreaded fever, apparently typhus, was endemic. Education for the most part took the form of banning the native language from classroom and playground in order to impart as much English as could be learnt by rote in the children's five years of schooling.

Escape from these conditions was only to be made by seeking employment elsewhere. For an islander this usually meant the armed forces or the merchant marine, where one could get by with a minimum of English; a job on a mainland farm where Gaelic was spoken; or emigration to Canada, where many Gaelic speakers had already settled. Angus MacLellan chose a combination of the army and the farm, first joining the Second Battalion of the Queen's Own Cameron Highlanders (the Militia) at Muir of Ord in June 1889, and then engaging to work for a big farmer in Perthshire, Mr Robert Menzies at Tirinie.

These were the days when Scottish farm-workers engaged by the six or twelve months' 'term' with farmers at hiring fairs, which were held in all the principal country towns in Scotland, including places like Stirling, Perth and Inverness. In the 1890s, Scottish agriculture had entered on a prolonged spell of depression. A skilled unmarried farm-worker's wages were then about fourteen to eighteen pounds for the half-year, plus lodgings in a bothy, that is, an outside building near the farm, where the accommodation might consist of a bedroom and a kitchen, with no water laid on, and, of course, no indoor sanitation. Oatmeal, milk, potatoes and coal were provided by the employer, and the workers were expected to do their own cooking, though on the better farms they would get their meals in the farmer's own kitchen. As late as 1939 this system survived in many parts of Scotland, though by then the cash wage was about five or six times higher. Admittedly, pay in the old days was in real gold sovereigns that would keep their value, and tobacco cost only threepence-halfpence an ounce and whisky three and sixpence a bottle, but hours were long, work had often to be carried on in very disagreeable weather, and comforts were few.

Angus MacLellan worked, mostly as a ploughman, on four mainland farms between 1889 and 1902; for Mr Robert Menzies at Tirinie from 1889 to 1892 or 1893, for Mr Tommy MacDonald at Borenich on Loch Tummel-side for a year, for Mr Edward Kane at Rowardennan on Loch Lomond-side from the spring of 1895 until Martinmas 1897, and for Mr Fraser of the Dalmally Hotel around 1898 to 1901.[4] As conditions then went, he could be considered fortunate in most of these situations. Work was hard at Tirinie but the farmer and his family and his employees formed a happy community there and Angus learnt a good deal in a district where the standard of farming has always been high. At Borenich and Dalmally he had exceptionally good masters and got meals with the household, not having to cook in the bothy. At Rowardennan his fellow-workers were not so compatible, some seeing fit to try to take advantage of one they thought a raw Highland lad—but catching a Tartar in the process. (There was no Gaelic at Rowardennan.) Here he decided to leave in consequence of being involved in unpleasant strife between his employer and his employer's son, otherwise, he says, there was little coming between him and his master, though it can hardly be said that the latter appreciated Angus's service and fidelity when the time came for parting.

Boyhood on Uist in the bad old days, young manhood in the Militia and on mainland farms, returning to Uist, where the Crofters' Act of 1886 had brought emancipation to the small tenants, in his prime to look after his parents and follow the livelihood of a crofter-fisherman, that is Angus MacLellan's story; and thanks to the skill with which he had learnt the art of the traditional Gaelic storyteller, it is told with a vividness, wit, dialogue and characterization that many a professional novelist might envy. Throughout the quiet strength of character and constant good humour of Angus himself under feudal conditions are always in evidence.

Angus was famous in Uist for his skill in handling sheep and horses, and once his family became landholders, in 1907, their conditions began to improve. After his parents died, Angus went to live with relations at Frobost, a few miles from Loch Eynort; until a few years ago he used to return to his old home for a few weeks every summer to look after his sheep. Today, a very youthful ninety-two-year-old, he lives in well-deserved comfort with a married niece, and his name is now well known to folklorists through the many valuable recordings he has made of Gaelic folk-tales, ballads, and songs for the late Dr Calum MacLean of the School of Scottish Studies and for the writer, a reputation which is also shared by his sister, Mrs Campbell, known in Gaelic as 'Bean Nill'.

In fact, the recording of this autobiography arose directly out of the preparation of translations of forty-two of his traditional stories for publication by the writer. When the selection had been made, Angus MacLellan was asked to record something of his own story as an introduction. This was done; and it was soon followed by a great many more reminiscences. These were recorded on tape in Gaelic over a period of more than a year, and were not related consecutively; therefore, their exact chronology is sometimes uncertain, but the story they reveal is clear enough.

Following the transcription and translation of the greater part of this material, in the autumn of 1960 I took advantage of being on the mainland for agricultural sales to drive around the countryside and visit the farms and hotels where Angus MacLellan had worked more than sixty years ago. None of these is now occupied by any representative of the families that had it in Angus's time, but in Aberfeldy I found two sons, Duncan and Alfred Menzies, and two daughters of Angus's first employer, Robert Menzies at Tirinie, who remembered Angus well although they had not seen nor heard from him for over sixty-five years. Both Duncan and Alfred Menzies figure in Angus's story about Donald Smith's purse

(p. 46), but neither of them could recollect the incident. Mr Duncan Menzies, and also Miss Mary MacIntosh, post-mistress at Camserney near Tirinie, gave me interesting information about persons mentioned in Angus's reminiscences of Tirinie.

Tirinie farm itself was sold some time ago, and the dwelling house has been separated from the farm, which is now joined to another. Borenich stands as it did, a picturesque site beside the road on the north side of Loch Tummel. The Rowardennan Hotel, a building of great character which is well known to lovers of Loch Lomond, has changed hands several times since Angus's time, and is now modernized. Farming has been given up, and a good deal of the neighbouring land has been taken for trees by the Forestry Commission. The little farmhouse of Ross, three miles to the south of the hotel, so often mentioned in Angus's reminiscences, has been sold off as a summer residence, and is now surrounded by birch trees that have grown up since Angus's time. Two of his acquaintances survived in the district—his friend Johnny MacIntyre, living near Aberfoyle, but unfortunately impaired in health and memory, and Alec MacGregor at Gartocharn, the son of the gamekeeper, one of the lads whom Angus caught when he was keeping watch for the poachers (see p. 90). Mr MacGregor, who died in the autumn of 1961, gave me interesting information on what had later become of several persons mentioned in Angus's Rowardennan reminiscences. The Dalmally Hotel has been burnt down and rebuilt since Angus's time. I did not find any of his acquaintances in the district, but I knew well the 'lad from Canna' to whom he refers in his story about the tramp, Donald MacLeod; Donald later returned home to Canna and was working for me there from the time I went there at Whitsunday 1938 until shortly before his death in 1949.

Angus's reminiscences are told entirely in colloquial Gaelic, which differs a good deal from the more formal language of the traditional folk-tale. Indeed, his autobiography will be much the longest text in colloquial Scottish Gaelic. He is never at a loss for a word, even if it has to be Scots or an English word. Actually, such loanwords have often been a part of the language for much longer than the purists like to admit, and might well be admitted to literary use, as similar loanwords are in Welsh. As I hope to publish the Gaelic text of this autobiography, I am not adding many linguistic notes to this translation, which follows the recorded Gaelic text, except that a few unnecessary repetitions have been cut out, a few short passages have been transposed, and sometimes the words 'he' or 'the other fellow', etc., have been replaced by the names of the persons referred to.

It remains to record my thanks to the persons who have assisted me in various ways: to Angus MacLellan's niece, Mrs Patrick MacPhee, and her husband, for much kind hospitality while making these recordings in their home at Frobost; the Rev John MacLean, and the Rev Donald Mac-Dougall, for their hospitality and help in transcribing some difficult words and expressions from the tape; to Miss Annie Johnston for help of the same kind during a visit to Canna (the standard Scottish Gaelic dictionaries are quite inadequate for explaining the colloquialisms of a Hebridean dialect); and to Mr Duncan Menzies, Miss Mary MacIntosh, and Mr Alec MacGregor mentioned above, for interesting information about the old days at Tirinie and Rowardennan; to Colonel C. I. Fraser of Reelig for the very interesting discovery of the dates on which Angus MacLellan joined the Militia, and went to see the menagerie in Inverness; and to Mr H. D. MacIntyre, the present Factor of South Uist, for information about the dates of various incidents there.

J. L. CAMPBELL

Isle of Canna,
27th July, 1961

CHRONOLOGY

1869 July 4. Angus MacLellan born at Poll Torain, Loch Eynort, South Uist.

1869 July 13. Baptized at Bornish by Fr MacColl.

c. 1876. Manx fishermen visit Loch Eynort with rum.

c. 1878. The Land Raid on Calvay.

c. 1882. Fever epidemic at Loch Eynort.

1889 June 21. Angus went into camp with the Second Battalion Queen's Own Cameron Highlanders at Muir of Ord, assembling at Inverness.

1889 June 22 (Saturday). Angus went to see Bostock's Menagerie at Inverness.

1889 July 20 (Saturday). Probable date camp broke up—or 19th—after twenty-seven days' training.

Angus travelled by train to Oban via Perth.

At Oban engaged, along with Donald Smith, by Robert Menzies' shepherd, to go to Tirinie.

1890 November 28? The term at which Donald Smith lost his purse.

1891 September? Angus and Donald Smith take Mary Iain Dick to the Birnam Games.

1892. Robert Menzies got Glen Golandie farm.

1893 November 28? Left Tirinie to go to Borenich.

1894 November 28? Left Borenich to go home to Uist.

1895. Early spring. Went to Oban from Uist and was working building pier. His sister got married in Oban.

Late spring. Replied to Edward Kane's advertisement and got job at Rowardennan.

1897 November 29, Monday. Left Rowardennan after 2½ years. Returned to Uist for the winter. (This is a certain date.)

1898. Went to work for Mr Fraser at Dalmally. Was there when Boer War broke out.

1899. John Ferguson gave up tenancy of Bornish farm.

1900? Left Dalmally and returned to Uist.

1903. Ranald MacDonald tenant of Ormaclate farm died.

1906. John MacNiven got lease of Ormaclate farm.

1907. Nine Loch Eynort families became crofters; final order in 1908. Angus MacLellan signed with an X on behalf of the cottars; witnessed by Norman Robertson and James Coull.

1901. Charles MacLean left Milton farm.

1911. John MacNiven left Ormaclate farm.
Land Bill passed.

1912. Crofters and cottars summonsed to Lochmaddy over Dog Licences.

1

BOYHOOD ON SOUTH UIST

I AM 'Young Angus', the son of Angus, son of Hector, son of Donald, son of Calum, son of Donald; my people, Mac-Lellans, were always at Loch Eynort and Benmore. Some of them went to America, and I have been hearing from these since two or three years. But they are very distantly related to us as it is more than two hundred years since they left South Uist.

My father had neither croft nor land, he was only a squatter on the land of John Ferguson, the farmer who had Bornish. My father had to pay rent for every cow he kept. He was allowed to cultivate what he could dig with the spade, and that was not much. He was not allowed to keep a horse, either. He was paying two pounds a year for every cow he kept, and if he had a stirk, he had to pay a pound after the cattle sale for having kept it. He was only keeping the march between the farms of Bornish and Gearrabhailteas.

I got very little schooling. The school was at Howmore. My mother's brother lived there. I was two years and a bit more there. The schoolmaster was a man called MacLean. They used to call him 'Pocketty'—that was his nickname, because he used to keep saying 'Keep your hands out of the pockets'.[1] He was a very cross man, but a good schoolmaster, good at teaching. I fell ill, and was taken home then; I didn't get another chance. I was only about seven years old at the time.

I can remember things that happened when I was six or seven years old much better than I can remember something that happened yesterday. At this time, all the family were at home. I had three older brothers, Donald John and Hector and John; they were about the same size, the three of them.

In those days, boats used to come from Ireland to Loch Eynort to buy potatoes. This year a boat came from the Isle of Man, a smack; I had never seen such a big boat at the time. What did she have on board but rum for sale. They were asking two shillings a bottle for the rum; there were no customs dues on Man then. At that time there were plenty of potatoes at Loch Eynort, I believe that one man had as much as there are altogether today.

The Manxmen[2] were paying seven shillings a barrel for the potatoes. The farmer in Bornish, John Ferguson, put a lot of potatoes on board, and took five gallons of rum out of her, and my father took a gallon.

But one day when my father was away from home my brothers saw nothing better than to get a barrel of potatoes to sell to the owner of the boat in order to get rum. Well, no one would know about it, anyway. They managed to put a barrel of potatoes aboard, and they got seven shillings for it, and took two bottles of rum away, and a shilling apiece. But they didn't know where to put the rum, in case it was discovered that they had it. The peat-bank was a good bit away from the house, about four hundred yards up on the hill. My brothers used to be terrible for hanging back when peat had to be fetched; if one of them went to get it today, another had to go to get it tomorrow. But there was nothing better they could do than to hide the rum where the peat was on the hill; and when they went to fetch peat, all three of them used to go to get it, as it wouldn't do to let one go by himself in case he went too deep into the bottle of rum! So it was that every time the house was short of peat, and one of the lads was asked to go and fetch it, oh, all three would get up and go off together.

It puzzled our father very much how ready the lads had become to go and fetch the peat, compared with the way they used to hang back. No doubt they were ready, until the rum was finished; but when the rum was finished, they began to hang back again as they used to do before. At the end of the year our father learnt why they had been so ready; they told him themselves how they had got the rum off the ship, and had hidden it up where the peat was! Father didn't say a word to them, he only laughed at them when he heard what they had been up to!

Another time a boat came over from Ireland to buy potatoes. She came to Lochboisdale. An Irishman was buying the potatoes; he was giving seven shillings a barrel for them. He came down to Loch Eynort in a boat belonging to a man called Angus the son of Big James. They came down to Loch Eynort to get potatoes in the springtime.

At the time the people of Loch Eynort were at work cutting seaweed to manure the potato ground. A man called MacAskill was going out with his boat to cut seaweed, and Angus the son of Big James and the Irishman were coming in. The day was rather squally. Angus didn't have much ballast in his boat, and what happened but that he swamped her just coming in towards our house. Luckily MacAskill was going out towards them, and he saved them, and saved their boat, and brought them ashore.

When the Irishman had got things in order, they went to the township to see if he could get potatoes. Would they sell him any potatoes? Oh yes, that they would. He brought the boat up Loch Eynort then. He was happy enough since he had saved his money; it had been in a pocket of his jacket, and the jacket was on the boat, it wasn't even wet; it was in the bow. When they were pulling the boat ashore, he asked them to look if the jacket was in her. They said it was. They got hold of the jacket.

'Oh well,' he said, 'it's all right.'

(I remember well when they were drying their clothes, they were in our house, drying their stockings. The fire was in the middle of the floor then. They filled their stockings with hay and put them beside the fire like that, and they weren't a minute drying. I was then about nine or ten years old.

There were plenty of potatoes here then. We always had plenty of potatoes. There was Kerr's Pink and Champion and Prince, whatever kind that was. The people who lived on the east side of Uist were growing so many potatoes in those days, breaking in the land; they had plenty of potatoes, but they couldn't grow oats unless they broke in the land with potatoes first, and made the earth soft. They used to take the seaweed up on their backs, in baskets. Many a spell I spent at it. It was some job: it's surprising how happy the people were at it!)[3]

Calvay

As far as I can remember, I was eight years old at the time, and my brother John was at Bornish farm herding the eld cattle. My father was living on land belonging to Bornish; he had a piece set aside for him for growing potatoes and oats, and he had to pay five pounds rent for it. But when John Ferguson (the farmer who had Bornish) turned his cattle out to the hill, we didn't dare to turn them off our piece, but had to stand by the potatoes and protect them. John Ferguson's beasts were eating the grass though my father had to pay for it.

Things went on like that. One time John Ferguson was away. His sister was keeping house for him at Bornish; she was a widow, her name was Peggy. She wasn't good to the farm-servants. The lads were being given maize gruel and beestings with it, and they refused it. That was all they would get. Well, neither my brother John nor the other herdsman who was along with him would eat it; and as they wouldn't get anything else, they went off and left it there. They came out to our house together. My father was wanting them to stay until John Ferguson himself came back, and they wouldn't; they went and enlisted in the Militia. My brother only came back to Uist twice after that. He was working for a long time out by Inverness at a place called Strathearn; after a number of years he left there and went to Australia, to Queensland, and got on very well there. A son of his is living there yet.

John Ferguson turned against my father so much that he couldn't get to keep a beast at all, but 'clear out of the place altogether'. My father's cattle were cleared off then. Charles MacLean (the tenant of Gearrabhailteas) then gave us grazing for a cow, and potato land. There were nine houses in Loch Eynort altogether; we and two others were on John Ferguson's land, and there were six on Ranald MacDonald's land,[4]

Ormaclate, he had Ormaclate farm at that time. The people of Loch Eynort had no place to grow potatoes, so they went to Calvay, a long green island opposite our house. The Land League was at work, and people were making land raids then. My father went there with them; he didn't go the first year, but he went the second. The first year they were there, he didn't go there at all, but the next year he went along with them.

Well, they dug a lot of land there. They were taken to Edinburgh, and they got six weeks' imprisonment for breaking the law. They didn't dare to take anything more to do with the place, nor did they dare to go to lift the crop, but they could send people they paid to go there to lift it.

The day my father got an interdict to stay clear of Calvay, he had finished working there that day, and he didn't dare to go there again until it turned out that they could go to lift the crop, could send people there paid to do it. That is what saved my father, so that he didn't go to prison himself. They took eighty bags of potatoes off Calvay that year; wasn't that a lot? Every one of them got their crop off, but they didn't dare to go there again. Ranald MacDonald, Lady Cathcart Gordon's head factor, had Calvay then. The people were doing the place good, breaking in the land, land that was going wild, that wasn't producing grass or crops, until it was manured. I was nine years old at the time. I remember well how they were taking me over there, when they were spreading seaweed, to help fill the creels; that was all I could do. I was filling the creels for them, and they were carrying them on their backs.

When Ranald MacDonald gave up Ormaclate and left Uist, a Mull man called MacNiven took it. The people of Loch Eynort then petitioned Lady Gordon Cathcart to have a piece of the farm cut off as crofts for themselves. Well, they got that. The Congested Districts Board cut off little pieces of it into crofts at Loch Eynort, and they were a good bit better off than they had been at first. They got Calvay to themselves eventually, and they aren't doing much cultivation there today!

How We Used to Live

We mostly lived on potatoes and fish then. We used to have bread and tea in the morning, potatoes and fish for our midday meal, and porridge and milk for supper. There was not much meal coming to Uist then, compared with today. There were few houses without a quern. When meal became scarce with us, we used to harden part of our grain and grind it in the quern. That was the way we lived.

We were beside the sea, and there was no work to be had, and the only way you could get on was to take to the sea itself. I and everyone else in the family went away, and my father and my mother were left alone; when they grew old, I had to come home to be with them. I got on all right after I came home, things were not so hard as they had been at first; we were getting plenty of meal now, plenty of ships were coming to Lochboisdale, but as I first remember, only one ship was coming a week.

The light we used to have was fish livers melted down and burnt in lamps called 'cruisgeins'. There was no paraffin coming to Uist at all, nor word of it. The first paraffin lamp I remember coming here, the smell of it could hardly be endured at all, it was so strong. I think the kind of paraffin there was then was stronger than the paraffin today. There was a man at Peninerine called Ruairi mac Dhòmhnaill Òig, 'Rory son of young Donald', who had got a jar of paraffin. One night he was putting oil in one of the lamps. They weren't very well acquainted with paraffin, and however it caught, the jar went on fire, and Rory began to shout 'My God! Upon my soul! Paraffin! Put it out of the house!' He hardly managed to get the jar out of the house, and nearly set the house on fire before he did! It was a long time before he would allow paraffin there at all, the 'cruisgein' was back again, until the family grew up; when the lads grew up, they made him stop using it. That's the kind of light I remember seeing at first, there was no word of electricity or of Tilly lamps at the time.

There was a mill at Gearrabhailteas, and another at How Beag, there were two mills down there. We weren't sending

6

anything to the mill. We had a quern ourselves, and we were making do with our own grain, if we could spare it. But the people on the west side of Uist used to send plenty of grain to the mill, barley; we couldn't grow barley at all, only oats.[5]

The miller used to keep the seventeenth peck in return for milling; if he had seventeen pecks of grain, you would get sixteen ground, and he would keep the seventeenth; that's how he worked it. When the mills first started here, when the proprietor built them, the millers were not getting much grain then, and they couldn't keep the mills going. Then the regulation was made by the proprietor that everyone who owned a quern, must have it broken. It was then that the ground officers began to go through the houses breaking the querns, and the querns were thrown out into a loch down at Ormaclate beside the main road. That loch has never been called anything since but 'Loch nam Bràithntean', 'the Loch of the Querns'; there are plenty of them yet in the loch. That was when they stopped using querns. But as for the people who lived on the east side of Uist, they weren't sowing much then; they weren't sowing barley then, it wouldn't grow for them.

The Fever

When I was young (I was about thirteen at the time) one of my brothers was a shoemaker, and he was working in the Isle of Skye. He caught the fever on the Isle of Skye. He didn't realize what was wrong with him at the time, but he came home, and when he got well after coming home—I understand that he had got over the worst of the fever before he came—he went back to the Isle of Skye. After he had gone back—he hadn't been gone long, only about a week—my brother Hector who was at home fell ill. The one who was a shoemaker was called Donald John.

We had a doctor called MacDonald, who lived at Dremsdale. The doctor was sent for, and he said that Hector had the fever. The doctor went away. Only a few days after he had gone, two of my sisters, Mór and Peigi, fell ill with the fever. Three of us were ill then. But my father and mother were all right. Then my father fell ill. I was happy enough as long as

7

my mother was up, but unfortunately she herself fell ill, and the five of them were ill together, and there was no one to look after them but myself. No one was coming near them or near the house. I had to fetch peat from a good distance, and I had cattle to look after, too, and I had no one to help me.

Well, the doctor used to come fairly often. Every day that he came he used to say to me 'don't be afraid at all, I don't believe you'll catch it. But put out every drop of water that's indoors at night, and bring in fresh water'.

I was all right as long as my mother was afoot, but when she herself fell ill, my heart broke, and I'm sure I wept enough tears to have washed my clothes with sorrow when I had no one left to help me. Anyway, things turned out like this; and they were allowed to have nothing but rice and milk. Well, we had no milk, we had only one cow in milk, and I'm sure I went to milk her pretty often. Every time I went to milk her, I would get a jugful of milk from her. And I used to go every day over to the head of the loch to get milk from the MacRaes' house; they were very kind to me, their mother wouldn't think of putting a drop of milk in their tea, but kept it for me until I came for it. Things were hard enough for me; when I got wet with the rain, I had only the clothes on me to wear until they dried on me, and at last my skin broke out in a rash.

But anyway, the first to recover was the one who had first fallen ill, Hector. He got up and used to come to the fireside, that was all he could do. Then my sister got up, and I was a little better off then; but they couldn't do anything. My mother and my father were the last to recover; it was a very long time before my mother got up. I was wearing the same clothes for six whole weeks, I'm sure, without a change at all but just as the rain would leave me and as I used to get dry at the fire.

It was the happiest moment in my life when my mother got better. None of them were the worse for it. I got over it. But a few years afterwards, these MacRaes were going to Benbecula, to a place called Creagastrom—there are descendants of theirs there to this day. When they were making their flitting going over to Benbecula, they had a servant girl, a cousin of theirs, called Mary MacRae, and while they were

8

flitting, she went for a day to Donald Ferguson's house on the south side of Lochboisdale. When she left there, during the night they had to go with their cattle to Benbecula, and unfortunately what happened but the poor girl fell ill in Benbecula, and caught the fever herself, and died in Benbecula.

After her death, when she had been buried, James MacRae and his brother Donald Bàn came over to Loch Eynort to take the thatch off the house so that they might take the beams and rafters to Benbecula. What happened but James fell ill at Loch Eynort. There was no bed nor anything in the house, they had taken the beds away; he could only make his bed on the floor. His brother was looking after him. One day my mother was baking, and she had been churning. She told me I must go over to the MacRaes' house with milk and bread and butter, since they themselves had been so kind to me.

'You go over,' she said, 'to where James is, but take good care you don't go in; even if God saved you before, take care you don't go inside again.'

'Oh, I won't,' I said.

She filled a basket with bread for me, and gave me a pail of milk, and put everything she had in the house in the basket. I went off, and when I reached the MacRaes' house, I went into the stack-yard and whistled. No one came out. I whistled again, pretty hard. No one appeared. Well, I said to myself, 'why am I waiting here? I've no reason to wait. I won't catch anything'. I entered the house. When I went in, I found only James; he was in bed in the kitchen on the far side of the fire, and his bed was on the floor. When I disappeared he said:

'Oh, thank God there's someone who'll come in though I were dead!'

'Indeed there is,' I said. 'Where is Donald Bàn?'

'Oh, he went to see if he could get milk.'

'Are you thirsty?'

'Indeed I am.'

'Oh well,' I said, 'I've plenty of milk.'

I went and poured the milk into a vessel for him, and put some water in it, and gave it to him. When he had drunk it he said:

'Oh, may your soul and the souls of your people be rewarded for that in heaven; but I hope to God you won't catch anything I have.'

'I won't,' I said.

I went and sat beside him, and stayed there until Donald Bàn came; he sent me out of the house.

'Oh, away with you,' he said, 'for goodness sake get out of here. Why did you come in?'

'Tut,' I said, 'I won't catch it, anyway. If I would, I'd have caught it long ago.'

Donald Bàn sent me out; and James said that the worst was over, so glad he had been to see me when I came in; and he recovered all right, and I didn't catch the fever, but I was low enough before the last of them got over it!

How I Found My Seven Hoggs

One time my father and MacAskill were sending away sheep to Glasgow. I was only young at the time. I was sent with Johnny MacAskill—he was a good bit older than I was—with the sheep to Lochboisdale. We didn't have many sheep then; we had only seven hoggs. With wool so scarce we used to shear the hoggs at weaning time, and we used to pen them in the winter, keeping them in at night, and letting them out by day.[6]

Sheep used to be smeared then, dipping them hadn't been heard of. When we were going off with the sheep, we heard the shepherd over on the other side of the house gathering sheep which he was taking in for the smearing; and what the pity did he take with him but our hoggs along with his own sheep! Well, Johnny and I kept on to Lochboisdale.[7] When we arrived there, we were waiting all day until the steamer came. It was ten o'clock at night before it came. We put the sheep aboard, and were returning by the Lochboisdale road; everyone was asleep, there wasn't a light in a house. When we had come more than a mile from Lochboisdale, we met a mare grazing beside the road, with a colt along with her, a mare that belonged to a crofter called Ronald, son of John, son of Lachlan. There was nothing better than to catch the black mare and she'd take us part of the way!

We caught her. Her back was as sharp as a big saw. I went ahead on her, and we went into the road. Then her colt lifted its head, and neighed, and her mother answered her, and in came the colt after its mother. When they were going past Johnny, he caught hold of the colt and jumped on its back. The colt broke away off the main road to the south, and all I could hear was splashing in the peat hags. I was in on the road. Johnny went half a mile into the peat hags before he got to the main road, and all he could take to the colt was his cap around her eyes; but he never lost her.

We kept along then, and the mare and the colt were going like two lambs coupled together, until we got past the game-keeper's house up there. Then we broke away from the high road to find a dell where there was good grass, and left them there. 'Off you go,' said Johnny, 'when they're full, they'll go home; they're far better off than being beside the road there.'

'Ah, well,' I said, 'it's likely I'll have to come in here today yet to Gearrabhailteas to get the hoggs.' Charles Mac-Lean the farmer had a rule then, that every stray sheep that came in was to be kept in until someone came to get it, and its owner would have to spend a day lifting potatoes for it, to pay for the grass it had eaten. This was what I was afraid of, that I would be sent to lift potatoes, when the weather was so cold. But Johnny turned to me:

'Aha,' he said, 'they haven't smeared any of the sheep they gathered today, they'll only be in the sheds, we'll go and get them.'

'How on earth will we get them without a light?'

'We'll get them, my lad, I've got matches. Come on.'

We kept on northwards to Gearrabhailteas. When we reached the farmyard, the smearers used to sleep in a house just opposite the farmyard, called 'Patrick's house', where the manager who was at Gearrabhailteas once lived. We were going as quietly as we could, in case man or dog noticed us and thought that we were stealing sheep. We got into the big shed; it was full of sheep, separated by hurdles. Johnny took in the dog, and shut the door, and began to light matches, and I stood in the middle of the sheep. He would light a match, and raise his arm. The hoggs were easy to see, having been shorn.

I saw one of them, and made a dive at her, and Johnny opened the door, and she was put out, 'take whatever road you like'.

Well, we got four this way; then we had to go into the cart-shed. We went in there, and Johnny took the dog with him, and stood behind the pillar. Well, I got the three others there, and you may be sure that it was a while between getting the first and the last, with matches! When the last one was put out, I heard the noise of her going round the end of the barn in the mud; God knows what way she went by herself!

Then we went quietly down the road; we didn't care once we had got clear of the farmyard. When we had gone a bit of the road, Johnny turned to his dog. 'Go and get them,' he said. The dog went back. 'Goodness,' I said, 'do you think he'll find them?'

'By the Book, he'll find them, if they're on land in Uist!'

'They're on land yet, anyway,' I said.

'Well, then, he'll get them.'

Well, we stood a long time there, and didn't hear anything. We went on another bit, and stopped. Then we heard one bark to the south of us. The dog's way was that he wouldn't bark until he was driving them; then he would give one bark, and not a sound more. We stood a long time there, and we didn't hear the dog. It was no use for us to whistle or shout in case there was someone up who would hear us. We kept on until we reached the main road out at the bridge. We stood at the bridge there. Then we heard a bark to the west of us, as if the dog was down at Àirigh Mhuilinn. 'Come on,' said Johnny, 'step out!'

We kept on northwards, however, we didn't see the dog, or hear anything or any beast.

'My goodness,' I said, 'he's on the "machair"[8] now, he'll have every hogg on the "machair"!'

'I should worry! Come on! It's likely he can see us though we can't see him. He'll come yet!'

We went on down the main road, and didn't meet anyone all the way. When we were coming down to the cross-roads at Bornish, there was a gravel quarry there, and you, speckled dog, were sitting beside the main road, with the seven hoggs inside the quarry, open-mouthed and breathing like bellows!

The dog couldn't get a place where he could keep them, until he found the quarry!

'Ho, there you are, my fine fellow,' Johnny said. All we did was to go on past them. Johnny turned. 'Bring them with you, my lad,' he said. The dog then went into the quarry and took the hoggs out with him after us, until he left them at our house. That's as good a turn as I ever saw a dog do!

Catriana, Daughter of Calum the Shepherd

There was an old woman called Catriana Chaluim Chìobair, 'Catriana, daughter of Calum the shepherd'. One day she came out to our house to ask for fish, and she got a bag of fish to take away with her. When she was coming over the hill,[9] who met her but the shepherd, a Skyeman called John Beaton, a big half-wit. What did the fellow think but that she had wool that she had been collecting in the hill! He spoke to Catriana for a while, and then he said:

'Ah, I'm sorry you're afraid of me,' he said to her.

She didn't think anything of it at first, but then she stopped and said:

'Why should I be afraid of you, you rascal? Do you think it's someone else's goods I've got?' She threw down the bag. 'That's what I've got in the bag,' she said, 'fish I got from the good soul at Loch Eynort. You black thief, you!'

John Beaton turned and gave her two or three strokes with his stick. Off she went then crying to see Charles MacLean, it was he who was in Gearrabhailteas then. She told Charles (he was a Justice of the Peace) what John Beaton had done to her in the glen, how he had nearly killed her with his stick. John Beaton was summoned to court. Charles MacLean wanted to be as easy on Beaton as he could. Catriana was telling of the treatment he had given her, 'blue patches yet,' she said, 'on my skin where he hit me with the stick.'

'Oh, well, indeed, Catriana,' said Charles, 'if you had a witness for it, I'd let John see that he mustn't do the like ever again, that it would be a bad thing for him to touch you again, Catriana; but I can't do a thing to him since you haven't a witness for it.'

13

'I'd rather—' said John '—if I'd known that, I would have given her as many strokes again!'

'All I could do,' said Charles, 'was to turn my back on him, the other creature didn't notice what he had said; he condemned himself in front of me, whether I liked it or not, when I was trying to let him off!'

How My Brother Saw a Phantom Funeral

My brother Hector was staying in my mother's brother's house at Howmore. There was a man called Ian who was very good at stories. This night Hector was sent to fetch him, the houses were so close together there. Hector found him in MacIntyre the stonemason's house, and said he wanted him to go home to his supper.

'Oh, very good, Hector, my dear fellow,' he said, 'but I'd like you to go and shift the horses,[10] they're over in the Gearra-chrot on the other side of the graveyard.'

'I'll do that,' said Hector. The night was clear, with moonlight. He went to shift the horses, and when he had shifted the horses, there was a shower coming. It was autumn, and he went to a cornstack[11] (to shelter). He heard a slight murmuring of talk coming behind him. He looked, and he thought that all the people in the world were coming towards him from the north. He leant back against the stack, and they scattered around the stack, and came together again in front of him, and he saw their white faces and the white tips of their hands. They were talking all the time, but he couldn't make out a single word of what they were saying, and their faces were turned towards the graveyard.

How I was Fined for Shooting a Rabbit

I was the youngest of four boys in the family. As each one grew up, he went away, but I had to stay at home last. When I was about fifteen, my brother Hector, who was sailing, came home and gave me a gun. I used to go out with it pretty often.

The world was a hard place in those times. One day I went to the hill to try to get a rabbit, and I shot one rabbit. Charles

MacLean the big farmer at Gearrabhailteas had a fool of a shepherd who reported me to the gamekeeper, and not only to the gamekeeper, but to the factor as well. I was taken up to Lochmaddy[12] and fined two pounds or fourteen days in prison for the rabbit.[13] The Exciseman was at the court, and waited at the foot of the stairs until I came down, and when I came down he said to me, 'That rabbit was pretty dear for you.' 'Indeed it was.' 'Well, they treated you very badly, they might have left it at ten shillings. They couldn't have fined you more for a first offence. The best thing you can do is to take out a licence and give them their fill of work.'

'Very well, give it to me.'

The Exciseman took me into his office and gave me a licence, and when the steamer came to Lochmaddy I went aboard, and who was on board but my brother on his way home with a new gun for me, a double-barrelled gun. I was very pleased to see him. We were put together in the steerage, and when we reached Lochboisdale, I put the gun on my shoulder and walked down the gangway and up the pier with it; the lad who had been taken to Lochmaddy to be fined returned to Lochboisdale with a new gun! After that I used to go out in a boat on Loch Eynort not caring who saw me, killing plenty of shags, and though I had been fined two pounds at Lochmaddy, I took in what would pay it within the year!

2

THE MILITIA

How I Joined the Militia

THERE WAS no work to be had, so I started fishing lobsters with two others, Allan MacMillan and Donald MacLellan from Snaoiseabhal. Some days we did middling well, and others we were working at a loss. Then I enlisted in the Militia.[1] The night I went to join the Militia was the first night I ever spent away from home. We took the steamer to Lochmaddy, myself and six others, and when we reached Lochmaddy we had only a very little money between us, which we put together to buy tea and biscuits, hoping to make tea in some house or other. Behind the prison there was a neat little house with its door open, and we went over to it. A young woman came to the door. We asked her if we might brew a kettle of tea as we had had nothing to eat since breakfast at home that morning. (By now it was late in the afternoon.) She said we might, and asked us to come in. We went in, and put the kettle on the fire; but it wasn't long on the fire before an old woman appeared the worse for drink, swaying from side to side. She turned to the girl and asked her who were these men who were in the house? 'Oh, only people who've come in to make some tea.'

'They can't make tea here!' said the old woman. 'If they want to make tea they can easily find somewhere else to make it.' She took hold of the kettle and took it off the fire and put it on the other side of the room. 'What brought you in here?' she asked us. Not one of us was saying a word, only listening to her. The oldest of us, Duncan MacDonald, said, 'Well, it'll take someone stronger than you to put us out of here.'

16

'What sent you here rather than to any other house in Lochmaddy?' said the old woman.

'This was the only house we saw with its door open. If you had kept the door shut we would be outside yet.'

'Well, the door that let you in is the door that will let you out,' she said.

'We won't go out,' said Duncan.

'Oh, it won't take me long to find someone who'll put you out.'

I didn't care for the way things were going, so I got up and went out to the end of the house without a word to see if there was any other house we might go to make tea. Then I saw the old woman come out of the door and go to the other end of the house. The girl had gone into the small room[2] in the middle of the house to go to bed. I thought I would slip in and ask her where we could make ourselves tea, and I did so.

'Oh,' she said, 'if you go a bit farther on, about half a mile, you'll find plenty of places where you can make tea, and somewhere to stay. I'm very sorry I couldn't make tea for you.'

'Is that your mother?' I asked.

'Oh, no.'

At that moment whom did I hear coming into the house but the old woman. I was terrified she was coming into the small room, so I blew out the candle. She went into the kitchen. 'Aren't you the most useless men I ever saw?' she said. 'Why didn't you go away along with the lad who's with you to the house over there where he's by himself?'

When they heard this, they all got up and went out. When they had gone out, the old woman slammed the door and locked it. 'Ho, rascals!' she said, 'that'll keep you out to-night. What did you let them in here for?' she shouted to the girl.

'Oh, they only came in to make tea; they had their own tea, they only wanted somewhere they could make it.'

'Upon my soul,' I said, 'is she coming in here?'

'Oh no, she's going to another room,' said the girl.

'How shall I get out?' I asked.

'I'll let you out when she goes to sleep.'

The old woman was a good while at the fireside before she

went up to the other end of the house. The girl was waiting to let me out. When she thought that the old woman was asleep:

'Come into the kitchen now, and I'll see if I can make you a cup of tea.'

'I'm afraid she'll get up.'

'She won't get up, she's asleep.'

I went into the kitchen. The girl put a chain on the fire, and I got tea. Then I went off to see if I could find the others. I went on to the pier. There wasn't a sign of any of them, until I heard a noise over at the back of the pier in an old carpenter's shed. I went over, and there they were. It was a frosty night and they were lying on planks in the shed there, white with frost. Then they started damning and cursing me, 'Where were you, we were looking for you since night came!'

'Where was I but in the small room along with the girl!'

'You were *not*!'

'Yes I was. Why did you heed the old woman when she told you I was in yon house by myself?'

'Good heavens! We were looking for you since nightfall, and you in the small room along with the girl!'

The steamer came at six o'clock in the morning, and we got tea when we got aboard her. Then I went to join the Militia.

Pack Drill

When I was in the Militia, if you did anything wrong, you were given pack drill. There was pack drill every night; if you did anything wrong, you had to go to it, in your kilt and red jacket, with your knapsack on your back, and your rifle and bayonet. You would be drilled for two solid hours, like training a horse.

Once I was coming up to the camp in the evening. A dozen of the soldiers were being given pack drill by the sergeant of the guard. They were drilling in a hollow like a quarry, and the sergeant was standing above them, and would shout to them 'Quick march!' When they were at the foot of the slope, he would shout 'Double, double, double!' They ran up the face of the slope, and when they were at the top, he would shout 'Halt! About turn! Quick march!' and then they would double up the other side of the hollow.

I stood watching them. There was a man called Duncan MacDonald there who was along in the same tent with me. His two feet were so big they were like fishing boats, and there were no boots in the barracks that would fit him until they were made to measure. When I saw him doubling up the face of the slope with sweat running down his cheeks, I burst into laughter watching him. The sergeant noticed me; he was on the other side of the hollow, and he shouted to me. All I did was to turn my back and make off. Then he shouted again, and I didn't let on I had heard him.

He came after me. I made for the camp. Quick as he was, I was quicker, and I was amongst the tents before he had got round the hollow. I zigzagged between the tents like a swallow until I got a tent between him and myself, and then I went into another tent. I threw off my jacket and sat on a bolster that was in the tent. The sergeant was coming along the tents looking in. He came to the door of the tent, and looked in. I looked him in the eyes. He went on; he hadn't spotted me at all.

'Well,' I said, 'that fellow nearly caught me.'

'Was he after you?' said a lad from Lewis who was in the tent.[3]

'Indeed he was,' I said.

'What did you do wrong?'

'Nothing, but I stood watching the men he had at pack drill.'

'Oh, it's a good thing for you he didn't catch you, or else you'd have been the last one to get off,' he said.

I got clear of the sergeant. I never had to do pack drill!

One day we were drilling, and the day was terribly hot. The Commander was giving us orders, and we were drilling, until at last we were nearly exhausted. There was a stream of sweat running off me down to my boots. At last we became so tired we didn't know what orders we were getting, and we weren't keeping in line at all. There was a sergeant called Robertson, who was very bad-tempered. He had a cane in his hand, and he came around and gave a swing with his cane and

the cane flew out of his hand and struck me in the stomach—
I was in the front line. The blow left me dazed and I fell out
and sat down on the ground.

The company halted and the sergeant-major came over to
me. 'Get up,' he said.

'I can't just now,' I replied.

He stood beside me. After a moment he said, 'Get up. I'll
help you.'

He caught me by the hand, and I got up on my feet. He
took me over to my place in the ranks. 'Stand there.' I stood
in the rank where I had been before.

After a short time our company sergeant came over.

'What's your name?' he said.

I told him.

'What's your number?'

I told him. He wrote it down.

'Well,' he said, 'you'll have to do pack drill tonight at six
o'clock, with your knapsack, rifle and bayonet, kilt and tunic
—and take care there's no mistake about it, that you're there
at six.'

It was useless for me to say anything; I didn't dare to
answer him, while I was standing in the ranks. But when we
returned to the tents he came over to my tent. He called my
name at the door. I went out.

'Take care you're out at six o'clock for pack drill,' he said.

'All right,' I said, 'but I'd like to find out the reason why
I'm being sent there.'

'Well, it's my job to tell you to go there,' he said.

'Well, it's my job to ask you why you're sending me to it.
Are you going to send me to pack drill because your cane
struck me today while I was in the ranks?'

Oh, he didn't listen to another word from me, he was off to
see the officer. He reported me for having been insolent to him
in the tent, and said I deserved to get a week in the cells.
There was a lad from North Uist, Johnny MacDonald, standing in the door of the tent; he was the tent corporal. The
officer called him. The officer was a son of Lord Lovat.

'What tent are you in?' he asked.

'I'm in number one tent.'

'Is that the one MacLellan's in?'

'Yes,' said the North Uist man.

'Were you in the tent while he was speaking to Sergeant Robertson?'

'Yes.'

'Was he insolent to him?'

'I didn't hear him being insolent to him, he only asked him the reason why he was being sent to pack drill.'

'Was that all he said?'

'That's all I heard him say, sir.'

'Well, tell him to come out and I'll tell him what the reason is.'

The North Uist man came in. 'The officer wants you to get ready for pack drill, he'll tell you the reason,' he said.

'Very good,' I said. I packed up the knapsack and cleaned everything and went out with my rifle and bayonet, and stood in line. I'm sure there were at least thirty-six for pack drill that evening. I stood at the left end of the line. The officer came with the sergeant-major along with him. He began at the right asking the men one by one 'why were you sent out tonight?' Oh, one man had talked in the ranks, and another hadn't been properly dressed, and another had had dirty buttons; every man had a reason until he reached me. 'Why were you sent out?' he asked.

'I don't know,' I said.

'Don't you know at all?'

'No, sir, unless it's for having been knocked out of the ranks today by the sergeant's cane. Unless it's for that. And if that's the reason, it's the last pack drill and the last drill for me, if I can buy myself out!'

'That's not so, sir,' said the sergeant-major, turning, 'but because you weren't smart at drill.'

'I don't know,' I said, 'I'm as smart as I've learnt to be yet.'

'Ah, well,' said the officer, turning away, 'off with you, go back, you won't have to do pack drill tonight. Get everything clean for tomorrow.'

All I had to do was to go back. The company sergeant didn't dare to say a word. He never opened his mouth! He got the chance to send me to pack drill once or twice after that, but he didn't do it, he let me off!

The Time the Menagerie Came to Inverness

When I was in the Militia, a menagerie came to Inverness,[4] Humboldt's Menagerie it was called. There was every kind of animal in it. We got to see it at half price as we were in the Militia. We walked all round inside; there was every kind of animal there; those horses from Africa, the zebras, were there, there were camels and dromedaries, elephants, tigers, and bears there; every kind of creature was there, including lions.

A young girl came then and stood at the top of the stairs; her bosom was covered with medals, and she had knee boots on. The manager said:

'That young girl is only seventeen years old, and she's the smartest girl in the world. The medals you see on her she got for training wild animals.'

She went down then. There were two lions in the cage. The manager went and got a chair and gave it to her. She opened the cage and went in with the two lions; she had a whip in one hand and a revolver in the other. She had names for the lions as you'd have for a dog. She called their names, and told them to go around her, and to jump to the end of the cage. She raised her leg towards the front of the cage, and told them to jump over it. One after the other the lions went round her and jumped to the end of the cage and then jumped over her leg.

Then she told them to lie down. They lay down over in a corner of the cage, side by side. She next went and took a black handkerchief out of her pocket and tied it herself behind her head, and sat herself back in the chair as if she were asleep.

'Well,' said the manager, 'now you can ask her anything you like, and she'll tell you the answer.'

Nobody asked her anything.

The manager went and turned his back to the cage and put his hand in his pocket and took out a penny. 'What's this' he said. She said it was a penny.

'What's the date on it?'

She told him. He put it in his pocket. Then he took out a shilling. 'What's this?'

'A shilling.'

'What's the date on it?'

She told him. Well, this went on with the spectators. The manager put his hand on each one he encountered. 'What's this?' She would say whether it was a man or a woman or a boy or a girl, or what sort of person it was, or what was their trade, or what they were. There was a lump of a fellow there, no distance from me; I and a lad from Stonybridge[5] were standing there side by side. The manager put his hand on this fellow, who had a grey suit on.

'What's this?' he said.

'A ploughman,' she answered.

'Married or single?'

'Married.'

'Any family?'

'Yes, three.'

'What's the name of his wife?'

'Janet.'

The manager went and took hold of the watch the fellow was wearing. 'What's this I've got?'

'His watch.'

'What's the number of his watch?'

She told him, figure after figure.

'Is she right?' I said, turning to the man.

'Oh, yes, indeed,' he replied.

The manager went over and put his hand on Ian, son of Ranald (my companion), who was beside me.

'What's this?' he said, slipping Ian's bonnet down over his forehead.

'His bonnet.'

'What's the number on it?'

She told it.

'What's the date on it?'

She told him the date when it was made, and the number inside the bonnet. 'Seven eighty-seven's the number.'

'Come away!' said Ian. 'Come away! the Devil himself is here!'

'Stop,' I said, 'let's see what else she will do!'

'No,' he said, 'come away from here!'

I had to go off with Ian, and I didn't hear what else she did, but a big enough crowd collected around her. But I said to myself, 'since you've told that, you could tell anything!'

3

TIRINIE

I Engage with a Farmer

WHEN CAMP broke up, I engaged with a farmer near Inverness. My brother John had been near Inverness himself, and had engaged with a farmer, and had had to leave him at half-term.[6] I found this was the same farmer I had engaged with! He had given me half a crown as airles money, but when I found that this was the man I had engaged with, I'd sooner have jumped in the sea than go to him! I didn't know how in the world I could get clear of him. He had promised to meet me at seven o'clock in the square,[2] and I didn't go. I and some others decided to take the train and go to Oban by Perth; if there were enough of us it was likely we would get to go at half fare. We went to the station and asked the stationmaster what it would cost to go to Oban.

'Twenty-one shillings. But if there were fifty of you, you'd get fishermen's tickets at ten and six.'[3]

'Oh, we'll be here, and more than fifty of us!'

'Very well, be here at ten to ten, and then you'll get them at ten and six.'

We went to the station when it was near the time, and when the office opened, we crowded round the window asking for the tickets. Everyone who got a ticket ran to the carriage. There weren't more than twenty of us altogether! But alas, when I got to the carriage, whom did I see in the station but the farmer I had engaged with looking for me, to catch me. I hid until the train left. That's the only time I ever kept something that belonged to another man, the farmer's half-crown!

After we reached Oban, I engaged there with a farmer to go back out to Perthshire. The farmer whom I engaged with was called Robert Menzies.[4] He was farming Tirinie, four miles out of Aberfeldy. I spent two and a half years with him, and during that time I never saw a day that kept us indoors.

The Snow-storm

Robert Menzies had a big place, two farms thrown together. There were five of us ploughmen there. There was a lad from Rannoch Moor called Archie Cameron along with me. Every time a bad day came I used to tell him that we'd have to get something to do indoors today. He would only look at me and laugh.

'You'll never see a day on this farm, Angus, that'll keep you indoors.'

'It must be some farm if a day never comes that will keep us inside.'

'Well, I've been here for two years, and I didn't see a day yet that kept us in,' he said.

Things went on like this. At the end of the autumn, at the beginning of the winter, there came a snow-storm from the north-west which blew down a fearful amount of timber. It blew down a plantation belonging to the Marquis of Breadalbane in which there were three thousand trees, and didn't leave one standing. It took a sawmill working for seven years before it was cleaned up.

That morning, when we got up, I was the first who went to the door. When I opened the door, a lump of snow came in. An oak tree which was beside the road outside, opposite the front door, had been blown down on top of the house, and the snow was piled up to the slates. I came back. The other lads were getting dressed.

'Well, Archie,' I said, 'you were saying you'd never seen a day on this farm that would keep you inside. I believe there's one today that will.'

'Take it easy,' he said, 'it's not seven o'clock yet.'

'Whatever the time is, you won't get out of here. There's an oak tree in the doorway.'

'Oh, we'll have to get out somewhere,' he said.

The lads came downstairs. We got out by the back window, which was at ground level, and got into the stable and began to make a tunnel in through the snow to the door so the women-servants could get to the cow-byre. It was the grieve who used to waken us, and that morning he hadn't come at all. We weren't in much hurry to go to our breakfast, thinking that there was nothing to be done anyway. Then we went in for our breakfast, and while we were at the table, who came in but the grieve.

'God bless me,' he said, 'haven't you had breakfast yet? Get a move on, it's seven o'clock!'

'Where are you going with your seven o'clock today?' I asked.

'Hark at that nonsense! Is there nothing to be done? Hurry up!'

He went out. When we had had our breakfast, we went out over to the stable. He was there joining chains and swingle-trees. He clapped his two hands together:

'You, Angus, you and Archie, harness your horses and yoke them to the snow-plough!'

'Is it snow you're going to plough today?' I asked.

'Yes,' he said. 'Get a move on!'

I didn't know what a snow-plough was, but I was watching the other fellow to see what harness he was putting on the horses, and I saw he was harnessing them for ploughing, so I did the same as he did. When the horses were ready, he went out of the door and I went out after him. We went around into the stack-yard. The grieve was there, tying swingle-trees and chains to the thing in the stack-yard that I had thought was a boat. He harnessed the four horses to it, and went inside it himself and sat on the seat in the middle, facing backwards. We were on the horses' backs, encouraging them; we couldn't walk beside them, the snow was so heavy.

The snow-plough was cleaning the path, and whenever the grieve saw we were going near to either side he was shouting to us 'Keep to the right' and 'Keep to the left'. We kept on, and then we got the farm road cleared; then we had to go to the fields where the hoggs were. We made paths through the fields then. The shepherd was there taking sheep out of a snowdrift beside the hedge.

Then we returned to the steading. While we unharnessed the horses and put them in to dry, some of the men were getting ready to take hay and turnips down to the hoggs, two others were at work cutting up the oak that was in the doorway. Archie and I were then told to go to the hill to look for cattle the boss had on the hill and put them inside. We went and found them beside a plantation there, surrounded by the snow, unable to get out. We got them down to the steading, and by the time we had got them into sheds and ridds, it was after dinner-time.

When we had had our dinner, we came out, and the order we then got was to harness the horses and start putting out manure—and the cold would have taken the nose off a monkey! I said to myself that since that day didn't keep us in, no other day ever would. That's what happened to me at that farm, I was two and a half years there and never saw a day that kept us inside. When it was freezing cold the boss used to say:

'Ah, it's cold, cold, today lads; what a good thing it isn't wet!' When it was pouring with rain he would say:

'Ah, it's wet, wet, today lads; what a good thing it isn't cold!' It was never going to be cold and wet on the same day! I thought that every place must be as bad as that, but the next place I went to, I didn't dare to go outside on a bad day, myself or the horses.

How I Learned to Work with Horses

The first time I worked with horses was at Howmore in South Uist along with my uncle, but I was only very young then. But I had a great notion for horses. Robert Menzies was ploughing up fifty acres every year, and had fifty acres under turnips, and another fifty acres under ryegrass. Well, I got the fourth pair of horses there. There was a fellow from Rannoch Moor called Archie Cameron who had the second pair, and the grieve, Big James Menzies, had the first pair.

Well, I spent a year with the fourth pair. Then Archie who had the second pair was leaving at the term, and the hiring fair day was getting near. Archie told me he was leaving at the term. 'Have you the chance of another place?' I asked.

'Yes,' he said, 'I'm getting a job with the hotel up there.'

'Oh, well, I think I'll leave myself,' I said.

'Well, I wouldn't advise you to do that at all,' said Archie. 'But if you stayed another year here, you could take the first pair anywhere.'

'Well, I'm not going to stay another year with the pair I've got,' I said.

'Well, I'm sure you'll get the third pair. I'm sure the man who's got the third pair will get my place. That's the one thing I'll miss when I leave this place, the horses. I was never working with their like. But you see if you can't get my place.'

'Oh,' I said, 'I'm afraid I can't do the job with them.'

'What's stopping you? You can make a stack as well as I can.'

'Oh, I'm not afraid of anything at all, except the drilling[5] when the turnips are sown.'

'Tut! you are doing things that are much harder than that. You'll only have to do the closing. Big James Menzies does the opening. You were closing some drills along with me down there just as well as I was. But see you get my pair when the boss speaks to you; I'm sure it won't be long until he comes around.'

A day or two after that, the boss himself came round. He went over to where I was.

'Well, Angus,' he said, 'hiring day is getting near, and we'd like to know who's leaving and who's staying. What do you say, are you willing to stay with the pair you've got for another year?'

'Indeed I'm not willing to stay another year with them,' I said.

'Will you take the pair Peter Walker has?' he said. Peter was the man with the third pair.

'No, I won't,' I said. 'I wouldn't want to take any pair here but Archie's if he's leaving.'

'Oh, well,' the boss said, 'I'm sure Peter Walker won't be very pleased at being passed over.' Peter Walker had been on the farm a year longer than me.

29

'Oh, all right,' I said, 'I'm not asking for them at all. You can give them to anyone you like.'

'Oh, well, I'm not keeping them from you. It would be a pity to keep back a lad who's willing to get ahead. But I'll see Peter Walker and find out what he thinks.'

He went over to see Peter. Peter engaged with the pair that he had. Then the boss came back over where I was.

'You say you want to take the pair that Archie has?' he said.

'Yes.'

'What wages are you wanting?'

'Well, I'll need to get the wages Archie was getting," I said.

'Oh, well,' he said, 'Archie was a good hand. Archie is fit to take the first pair on any farm.'

'Well, I'm sure that Archie wasn't doing anything but what I'll have to do, and so I must get the same wages.'

'Very well then,' the boss said, 'right enough, Angus.'

In the evening we went in. The men were talking about who was staying and who was leaving. Peter Walker said:

'The only man he needs now is a secondman.'

'He doesn't need a secondman at all,' said Archie. 'He's got one.'

'Who?'

'Angus there.'

'The devil! Has he done that to me? Upon my soul, if he's done it this year, he won't do it next!'

Never mind, things were going on all right for me until the time came to sow the turnips, and plant the potatoes. We had prepared a field just right for drilling. Well, there were two ploughs starting; the grieve was starting opening the drills, and the secondman was to close them behind him. I was at work spreading dung before dinner-time, while the grieve was opening the drills. I expected to be closing them after midday. When we went off to our dinner, the grieve said to me:

'You'd better go along with the women to spread the dung, Angus, and see and make them spread it evenly, and keep it low in the drills.'

I went off with a fork along with the women. When I went into the field I took a look behind me, and who was there but

30

the grieve and my pair of horses being worked by an old fellow called Johnston, an old farm-servant employed by the day, who used to work in the garden. Didn't this please the rest of the men! 'There's your secondman now for you! Why haven't you got your own pair? Off with you if you're a man, go and take them from him!'

Well, I wasn't going to—the man was a good sort and could give me the teaching of five years; he had always worked for farmers. 'Let him keep on with them,' I said, 'he's all right.'

When we stopped at nightfall, I went off to the bothy. Johnston only let the horses into the stable; he had nothing more to do with them. He took up his jacket and went off. The horses were standing in the stable in their harness. I was in the bothy making a fire.

The other men asked the grieve 'Who's going to strip the horses here?'

'What horses?'

'Angus's horses.'

'Where is he?'

'We don't know where he is, unless he's in the bothy.'

Big James Menzies came along and came into the bothy.

'What's the reason you haven't gone to strip and clean your horses?'

'They're not my horses,' I said. 'The man who was working them is the one who should have stripped and cleaned them.'

'Off you go and strip them!'

'I'll not move an inch,'[6] I said.

'I'll make you go!'

'You come in,' I said, taking hold of the poker, 'and I'll knock you down, big as you are.'

The row began. The boss was coming out going down to the byre. He heard the row at the bothy, and came up.

'What's going on here?' he said.

'What but Angus here won't go and strip his horses and they in the stable yet!'

'What's wrong?'

'What's wrong 's that he took my horses away from me yesterday and gave them to someone else,' I said, 'and I'm

31

not going to be a groom for another man here at all. I engaged
to work a pair of horses, not to clean and feed them for somebody else.'

'Did you take the horses from him?' said Mr Menzies,
turning to Big James.

'I didn't take the horses from him, I only asked Johnston
to close the drills with them, I knew he would close them
better than Angus.'

'Had Angus failed to close them?'

'I hadn't failed, I didn't get the chance,' I said.

'Well,' said Mr Menzies, 'I gave the horses to you, and I'll
take them from you if you don't work them; don't you let
anyone else take your horses as long as you're working them
yourself.'

'All right,' I said. 'Very well, let Big James go and strip and
clean them, since he didn't make the man who was working
them clean them.' I went back into the bothy.

But Johnston came the next day; he was thinking he would
be closing the drills as before. He asked the grieve:

'What'll I be at today?'

'Well, I'm sure you'll have to go to put out dung today,
there was enough of a row here last night because I gave you
Angus's horses.'

'There was no row,' I said. 'You made all the row there
was.'

'Did you ask him to give them to me, Angus? Did you?'
said Johnston.

'No, I didn't,' I said. 'How would you like to have that
done to you yourself?'

'If I had known that, I wouldn't have put a collar on them.
You keep your horses, Angus, and anything you want shown
to you, I'll show to you, you don't need to be a stranger.'

The grieve went off and harnessed his horses, and I went
down. Johnston went along with me. He closed the first drill
himself. 'That's them for you now,' he said. 'Don't go very
deep at all, just leave a little hollow on top of the drill; that's
the right way, don't put it over the top of the other side at
all.'[7]

Johnston went off. I was going at it as hard as I could.[8]

Johnston followed me until I had closed two drills. When I had closed two drills 'Go ahead,' he said. 'Big James never closed them better than that. They're all right.'

That's where I first learned to work with horses!

The Early Riser

This Peter Johnston had a house; he had no family, he and his wife lived a mile away from the farm. Every morning he would be in the stable before we had our breakfast; he was working by the day, mostly working in the garden. Peter Johnston's early rising used to be cast up to us; he only an old man, while we wouldn't get up—we'd do nothing but sleep. We were getting dispraised.

But once I and another lad, Donald Smith, were coming past Johnston's house; it was just after harvest on the farm. It was only about nine o'clock in the evening then, and oh! there was not a spot of light there. Peter Johnston had gone to bed.

'My word,' I said, 'it's no wonder he gets up early, when he's going to sleep at nine o'clock! But come and we'll shut the door, and he won't get out so quick tomorrow.'

We went over to the house. We got a stob and put it across between the two doorposts, and we got a piece of rope, and we tied it to the doorhandle and to the stob. We shut the light out of the windows with straw outside from the miller's stack-yard that was next door; we caulked them as well as we could, and we went off.

Next day when we got up, Peter Johnston had not come at all. Then we went to our breakfast. Peter didn't come. The boss asked 'Has Peter Johnston come today at all?' 'He hasn't come, we haven't seen a sign of him.' 'Well then,' the boss said, 'he must be ill; there must be something wrong with Peter.' We didn't let on, but next day, when we were at our breakfast, Peter came with his jacket under his arm. He came in and stood at the end of the table and he began to look at us one by one, smiling. When he looked at me, I couldn't keep from laughing. I burst out.

'Oh, you devil,' he said. 'I'm sure you had your share of it.'

'What was it?' I said.

'Oh, you don't know what it was! You know nothing about it! You black rogue! Who shut me in all day; wasn't it four o'clock when the miller came home, wasn't it he who let me out?'

'Never mind,' I said. 'You won't come so early again.'

He made fun of it and didn't take it badly. He was a very decent fellow. He never came so early again.

The Best Horse I Ever Saw

It was at Tirinie that the best horse I ever saw was, I think. There was a horse there which was four years old before harness was put on it. And it got three first prizes at the Cattle Show; every class that it entered, it got first prize. When it was four years old, they were going to put it in a cart. An oak tree was brought up to the field above the farm for the horse to be harnessed to, the first wet day that we wouldn't be doing much. The horse was in the stable. There was no harness in the harness-room of any use for him until his own harness had been made for him. His own harness came, and was hanging in his stall, and they were waiting until a wet day came so that we could go to train him.

Then we began taking in the turnips. A Lowlander, Bob Mellows from Crieff, came to work on the farm. There w s another horse, an old one, along with this horse in the stable. The grieve, Big James Menzies, said to Mellows:

'Go along and harness the black horse in the stable, and start taking up turnips.'

Mellows went off; now, he had never heard anything about the other horse. He went into the stable, and looked at this old horse, and thought that he shouldn't be harnessed anyway, there was nothing to him but bones, the poor old creature. He went and started to harness the other horse! He harnessed him and put him into the cart and went down the farm road with him. He wasn't noticed until he came into the gate of the field. Oh, the grieve uttered a yell when he saw Mellows coming into the field with the cart and the horse that had never been in harness before! He ran off to meet them.

34

'You blockhead, what made you take out that horse, that was never harnessed?'

'You rascal,' said Mellows, 'why didn't you tell me that? How could I know whether he'd been in harness or not? If I'd been killed, it would have been your fault!'

There was nothing for it but to fill the cart with turnips; then two men went with the horse up to the farm. The horse didn't put a foot wrong; even if the house had been tied to him, if he didn't take it with him, I believe, he'd have had to break something, he wasn't going to refuse at all! One day Mellows was putting out dung with him—the horse was so wise that he would keep his own side of the road without a man at his head, though he saw another cart coming towards him. One day Mellows was coming along behind him with a cartload of dung, and was filling his pipe, walking behind the cart, and I was coming up in the opposite direction. The horse hurried over beside the wall below the house. The wall was so high—there were stones in it extending from side to side. What did the horse do but stay too close to the wall and the wheel of the cart hit the guard of these stones. There was a crack; the next pull the horse gave, he took the two slings out of the trams, the saddle-girth broke, the saddle and the breeching stayed with the cart, and he had the two slings on his hames! The horse turned around on the main road to look at the cart! That was the best horse I ever saw harness go on.

The Mare that Came Home by Herself

Robert Menzies was keeping a shepherd in Glen Gomey,[9] while I was at Tirinie, called MacCallum. There was an inn a little way above the house there, where you'd get a refreshment any time you went there, it was so far from everywhere else; it was just half-way between Kinloch Rannoch and Aberfeldy. You could get a refreshment there even at any time of the night.

Mr Menzies kept a farm-servant up at the house (at Glen Gomey) along with the shepherd. The farm-servant was a fellow called Baldy Cameron, from Rannoch Moor. Mr Menzies had a brown mare, working in the farm where I was, here at Tirinie. Baldy Cameron and MacCallum used to go up some days to drink at the inn, leaving the horses outside; and when the brown mare grew tired of not being put inside, she would make for Tirinie. When we would go to feed the horses at eight o'clock in the evening, she would be standing in the stable. We used to let her inside. When we got up in the morning, there was no sign of her, Baldy Cameron would have taken her away.

The boss didn't know anything about it. But one time, unfortunately, he was going round the byres at eight o'clock, and when he went past the door of the stable, the brown mare was standing in the door. He came over to the bothy and went in. 'Is Jock Cameron here?' he said.

'He isn't,' we answered.

'His mare's standing in the stable door; you'd better let her in. Something must be wrong.'

We didn't let on at all. We let her in. Anyway, when we got up in the morning, the mare had gone; we could see no sign of her. Well, the boss had his suspicions. One day, it was raining. He went up to Glen Gomey, and went into the shepherd's house; and neither the shepherd nor the farm-servant were in. He kept on up to the inn, and there they were together, blind drunk! What happened was that he gave them the sack, he sent them both away.

The inn was kept by a widow, Mistress Lamont, who had two children. The shepherd wasn't married at all. What did he do then but go and marry the widow who had the inn, and he was far better off! That's how the matter turned out in the end.

The Time I Took Coal to the Kiln

Robert Menzies had another farm, a sheep farm, up in a place called Glen Gomey,[9] which was five miles away from Tirinie.

There was a lime kiln up on the top of the hill, and once I and the grieve and a fellow from Crieff, called Bob Mellows, were sent with carts of coal up to the kiln. We were to bring cartloads of lime down with us. But this fellow from Crieff was terribly heavy on sleep, and he was with the last cart. The grieve was in front, and I was after him.

When we were going past this farm in Glen Gomey—the horses used to work there sometimes—what happened but Mellows had fallen asleep sitting on top of his cartload of coal. The road was very rough and the slope very steep, and he had two horses with the cart, one on a trace, and the other pulling the cart. When the horses were opposite the gate, they turned in towards the steading and the wheel of the cart struck the gate-post, and the cart and the horses were turned upside down and Bob Mellows was thrown ten yards off the top of the cart.

We heard the crash behind us, and we stopped and looked round. One horse was on his back in the gate, with the other dragging him. The grieve went back, shouting to me to keep an eye on the horses. I stopped the horses, and the grieve went down. He unhitched the horse that was dragging the other horse, from the trace, and he untied the other, cutting the harness with his knife and letting the horse go loose. The horse's head had been cut in three places, but I don't think anything much had happened to the fellow who had fallen asleep, though he deserved it.

He went along then. When we were near the kiln, the man in charge of it was jumping around the kiln, with a big stick. We didn't know what in the world he was doing. The grieve went over to him and asked him what he was doing there.

'Amn't I chasing the devils?' he said, 'putting them inside the kiln? I've got them all in but one,' he said. He was in the blues! All we could do was to cope the carts there and then go back down. The shepherd whom Robert Menzies had in Glen Gomey was living in the house there. The grieve told the shepherd's wife, 'See and take in the coal, it will be useful to you; and sweep up the place.'

The broken cart was tied behind one of the other carts and we brought it down to the steading. The boss was not at home when we got back. The grieve put it at the back of the shed and pulled the two other carts up in front outside. The grieve wouldn't tell the boss anything if he could avoid it. The first day the boss was away from home, the grieve was going to send the cart to a carpenter to be mended. But unfortunately one day, when we were putting in turnips, the carts outside the broken one were taken out and we were at work with them. The boss came round and saw the broken cart there. He went down to the grieve.

'Who,' he said, 'broke yon cart at the back of the shed?'

'Oh,' said the grieve, 'that's an accident that happened to us the day we went up with coal to the kiln.'

'Who was with the cart?'

'Bob.'

'If he had paid heed to what he was doing, that wouldn't have happened. Why didn't you tell me about it?'

'What need was there to tell about it, when the fellow was alive?'

'It would be a small loss if he weren't,' said the boss. He went over to Bob and gave him a terrific scolding; but he didn't give him the sack, he left him there. A week afterwards we went to get the lime, and the man who had been putting the devils into the kiln, was all right that day, and we got the lime. That's how I left them.

Cattleman at Tirinie

I spent a winter fattening cattle at Tirinie. There were two byres, and where the manure was going, there was a dozen beasts there I had to feed, too. There were more than forty of them altogether. Well, there was not a day I was in bed later than four o'clock in the morning, and I wouldn't be clear until eight in the evening, between feeding and cleaning out the byres and everything else I had to do. I had to bruise oats for them in the mill, and I had to go a good way to let the water into the mill, it was driven by water; and I had to go again and stop it. With everything that was delaying me, my time would be running pretty short.

When seven or eight of them were fat and ready to go to the sale, I had to go with them, and I had to leave at four in the morning. The station was four miles away, and they had to be trucked at ten minutes to six in the morning. There was no one at that hour—four o'clock—to let them out of the byres with me but my dog. My dog used to sit in the farmyard watching me; every time a beast came out, it would bellow, and would be gone like a flash around the square.

I think the dog was watching every way they were going, and when I would let the last of them out, there was no sign of him. There were three farm roads leading to the steading, to the farmyard, and I wouldn't know which road the beasts would take. All I would do was to go down the track leading to the main road then and begin to whistle. I would hear a bullock lowing up between myself and the hill, and I would hear the dog bark, and he would come with perhaps two beasts, and sometimes he would come with one, but he wouldn't stop until he had caught the last of them and put him on the road in front of me.

Then he would keep down the road before me, and stand in every gap in the hedge in case one of them would go through. He would be at the end of every farm track coming down to the main road, 'none of you will go this way'. When I was going through the town, he was just the same in every opening on each side of the road, until I had put them into the pens down at the station. When I had got them trucked like that, I used to go up to the station, and Mr Menzies would have come with the machine; he wouldn't leave the house until twenty minutes before the train was due to leave. I would then take the machine home, and lift the dog into it, and I would have to go and fetch Mr Menzies at eight o'clock in the evening.

When I got home then (in the morning) I would be going hard at it in order to be ready early before the time came for me to go to the station. When I reached the station at eight o'clock, Mr Menzies would have arrived; then all I'd get, he'd say to me, 'Off with you now, there are beasts down in the pens, bring them home with you!' I would go down to the pens then, and there he would have as many brought back from Perth, pretty lean ones, and he would say 'take them back home with you now, and feed them, and leave them as fat as the ones that went away!'

I would be all night coming with them, and it would be morning before I got home. I would put them then into the ridd, and I would get about an hour's sleep before I went to the byres. I was this way until St Patrick's day. When St Patrick's day was past, there were no more beasts coming indoors, and those indoors were put out. I was well enough off for three weeks then, I only had eight in the byres, and all I had to do was to feed them until they were fit for the butcher. And when I got clear of them, I swore that I would never spend another winter feeding cattle again! The year after that Mr Menzies tried to put me indoors again, but I wouldn't have gone even if he had given me a hundred pounds.

He got a man up from Crieff, who stayed a fortnight before he left. Then he got a man down from Rannoch Moor, who stayed a week and then left. It was he himself and his son who looked after the last of them towards springtime, and I'm sure he came to me twenty times to see if I'd go in for them, and I'd get anything I asked; but even if he'd given me the farm, I wouldn't have gone to look after them again. And that's what happened to me and my grey dog, if it hadn't been for the grey dog, I'd have been in a poor way!

How the Tinkers Topped the Turnips

Mr Menzies used to sow a great deal of turnips every year, about forty-five acres every year, and there was a great deal of work in thinning and lifting them.

One year we were a bit behindhand getting in the corn and the hay. A tinker came round asking for work, for himself and the squad that was along with him. Mr Menzies told him he would get it, that there was a field of turnips of fifteen acres there, if they would top the turnips,[10] they would get seven and sixpence an acre for it.

'Well, all right,' said the tinker, 'it's a bargain.'

They came. I don't know how many of them there were, they were there both big and small; they had three tents in the field. They began in the morning. There was a moon, and they worked all night. Well, they took two days and a night topping the fifteen acres, and the tinker was at the door just before the boss came out, at the end of the second day. When he came out, he asked if the field was ready. The tinker said it was. Well, he wouldn't believe the tinker, he had to go down himself and see if they had been topped right, if the work had been done right. He went down; it had been done so well that it couldn't have been done better. The tinker got his wages,

40

and all we had to do was to cart the turnips home then, and there was work enough for us in that.

Gaelic in Perthshire

There was plenty of Gaelic in Perthshire when I was there. The Gaelic there, indeed it wasn't good. At the end I could understand every word they said, and I could speak their Gaelic just as well as they could. I can still remember their Gaelic, every word they had.

We call the place where we keep our stacks an 'iothlann'. Well, they called it a 'loin'. We call men cutting grass with scythes 'spealadairean' and they called them 'fàladairean'. Ploughing (which we call) 'treobhadh', they called 'crann-aireachd'. And carts, 'cairtean'—well, that's not correct Gaelic, 'cairtean' isn't the correct Gaelic at all, but they called them 'cùb'. And grass cut for drying, they called 'saoidh'; they called green grass, grass that was growing 'fiar', they called that 'fiar' right enough. There were very few words they had right compared with Argyllshire or Inverness-shire Gaelic.

They called a wall 'dìgean' instead of 'gàrradh'. Well, I think that was only something they got from English; they called it 'dìg'.

I could make more of their Gaelic than they could of mine; they couldn't understand me, they could make very little of it out, until I told it to them again.[11] One day we were at work threshing, and what happened but the feeding-bolt of the threshing mill broke. The grieve shouted to me from above— he was feeding the mill and I was down below at the grain— 'Go down to the dairy and bring me a brace ("burral") and some nails.'

I stopped. I didn't know what in the world a 'burral' was. 'Who's got that?' I said.

'Go along,' he said, 'Babby will give it to you.' Babby was the dairymaid.

'Is Babby going to lay a "burral"?' I said.

'Oh, the devil take you, you know the Gaelic for it, and you don't understand it.'

'I don't understand *your* Gaelic,' I said, 'your Gaelic couldn't be worse if you had learnt it from the crows.'

'Well,' he said, 'do you know what a brace is?'

'Oh, aye, aye,' I said, 'a "snìomhaire", for making holes. Oh, if that's what a "burral" is, I'll get it right enough.'

I went off along to the dairy then; I asked for what he himself had asked. Oh, Babby went at once and got me the 'snìomhaire', and handed it to me. I came back with it.

'Is that what you're wanting?' I said.

'It is,' he said. 'What do you call it yourself?'

'A "snìomhaire",' I said.

'A "snìomh"?'

'Not a "snìomh",' I said, 'but a "snìomhaire".'

'Oh, I can only let you be,' he said.

That's how I was getting on there; they were very fine people; big strong men. Before I left they could understand every word I said, and they were very willing to learn my Gaelic, too. They said it was much better than theirs.

I didn't know much English myself when I joined the Militia, but I could understand more than I could speak. It was difficult at first. But the time I spent at Rowardennan helped me a lot; I don't think I spoke three words of Gaelic as long as I was there, there wasn't anyone for me to speak to.

Ancient Monuments

One day we were working ploughing for Mr Menzies. There were no stones at all in the field I was ploughing. But the plough hit a stone in the middle of the field, and nearly knocked me down, it lifted me from the ground. I cursed the stone roundly. And who came up behind me but the boss himself!

'Tut, tut, Angus,' he said, 'what horrible language you're using!'

'It's no wonder,' I said. 'What damned stone's this here?'

'Ha,' he said, 'there's more than that there. There are three others there. You take care.'

'Ho, it's loosened,' I said.

'Oh, yes,' he said.

'Why on earth didn't you take it out?'

'Oh,' he said, 'you're not the first man to say that. We mayn't do that. It's in the lease that we mayn't move one of those old things.'[12]

He went and showed me where the stones were, they were as if they had been drawn into a cross. They were like flat gravestones, and there was only about four inches of earth on top of them. And there was a big pointed stone in the field a short way from the river.

'There you are,' he said. 'Those stones belong to your religion.'

'What connection have they got with any religion?' I asked.

'Did you see the big stone that's in the field down beside the river?'

'I did,' I said.

'What do you call that stone?'

'I only call it a stone.'

'Well, we call them the "Clachan Ìobairt", "Offering Stones",' he said. 'There's where the priests used to say mass when they were outlawed here.'

'Aye, aye,' I said.

'Have you seen the big cross up at Dull?'

'I have.'

'That's the cross that was on top of the church then; there was a college there, at first. They don't dare to move it.'[13]

Well, the stone was beside the road just as if it were going to fall, standing on one arm just beside the road. I believe it was three tons in weight, the size it was, of granite.

'Well,' I said, 'that's difficult to prove today.'

He began to laugh. 'Indeed,' he said, 'I don't think there's any here today [of your religion] but yourself and Donald Smith.' (Donald came from Stonybridge in Uist.)

There was a good harvest there every year; wet or dry there would be a good harvest in Dull.

Divination

Peter Johnston used to tell stories about a young fellow at Aberfeldy, at an hotel, who was going home one night; his mother's house was up near the head of Loch Tay. This time, he didn't get home; and his mother thought he was in the hotel. When she came into Aberfeldy and asked why he had not come home, they told her he had left for home two days before, and that they hadn't seen anything of him since. Then they began to look for him. They knew he wasn't alive, or someone would have seen him. There was no sign of him, alive or dead.

There was an old woman up on Rannoch Moor, who was said to be a seer. Two persons went from Aberfeldy to see the old woman, and told her what had happened, that the lad had been lost, and no sign found of him. The old woman went along to her room, and came back after a little time.

'Well,' she said, 'I was never in Aberfeldy; but there is a bridge over the river on this side of the town, and there are three pillars under the bridge. The lad has been drowned, he fell into the river a quarter of a mile to the west of the bridge, and he went under the span of the bridge that's nearest to the town, and he's in the pool there. There's an oak tree growing on the bank of the river. When it's twelve o'clock the shadow of that tree will be over his body. You try for him there.'

The men came back. The next day, they started to look for him, and when it was twelve o'clock, they tried in the shadow of the tree, and they found the lad where she had said. She had a daughter at home, and they used to say that the daughter was as good at divination as herself.[14]

Sir Robert Menzies and Sandy

Sir Robert Menzies the laird at Aberfeldy had a gamekeeper —he owned the land up to Rannoch Moor, and there were many poachers on his estate. There was one place down at Strath Tay, it was called, where no gamekeeper lasted any length of time, they were beaten up at night by the poachers. Sir Robert Menzies had a gamekeeper called Big Sandy, a big strong rough man; and he sent Sandy down to Strath Tay.

Sandy went down there; and wasn't capturing anyone. Sir Robert used to ask him if the poachers were troubling him. Sandy would say the poachers weren't troubling him at all.

Sir Robert was speaking to the other gamekeepers, and they were saying, 'Oh, good old Sandy isn't looking after the game there; if he was, he'd see the poachers just as well as we see them, and he'd recognize them too.'

One night Sir Robert thought he would go out himself, and would see whether Sandy was doing his duty. He took his gun with him. He went out above Sandy's house, and on his way past, he fired a shot. Sandy was in, and he heard the shot. He got up and took a big stick with him—he didn't take his dog at all—and went off after him. Sir Robert was going ahead, firing a shot now and again; but Sandy was overtaking him. Then Sir Robert saw Sandy, and when he saw him, he made as if to run away. Sandy was herding him down to the river Tay. When he had nearly caught up with him, Sir Robert turned round and lifted his gun to point it at him, but Sandy came at him with the stick and hit him on the side of the head and knocked him down where he was. Sandy jumped on his back and started beating and kicking him.

Sir Robert started to shout: 'Stop now, Sandy! It's me! It's me, Sandy! Stop, Sandy!'

'Oh yes, you b——, I know it's you, but I'll see you won't come again!'

He nearly killed the laird before he realized that it was he. Then he began to ask forgiveness, and he had to go with Sir Robert himself to the castle and leave him there, and Sir Robert spent a fortnight in bed. Sandy went home, and when Sir Robert got better, he sent for him. Sandy arrived.

'Well, here you are, Sandy,' he said.

'Oh, yes,' said Sandy, 'and I'm sure I didn't come to get crowned!'

'Well, I don't know,' said Sir Robert. 'I was to blame, Sandy, and not you. They were telling me that you weren't looking after game at all, and I was asking you many a time were the poachers troubling you, and you were telling me they weren't; but I don't wonder the poachers weren't troubling you if you were dealing with them the way you dealt with me.'

'That I was,' said Sandy, 'and worse. It was no good for me, if I caught a poacher, to give him up, or get him fined, that meant nothing to him; but if I caught a man I'd make sure he'd never come again; and that way nobody was troubling me.'

'Oh well, then, Sandy,' said Sir Robert, 'you won't be gamekeeper out there at all, but you'll be my head gamekeeper,' and Sandy got promotion, he got to be head gamekeeper, and Sir Robert had a great respect for him ever afterwards, and kept him always, until at last he got so feeble that he couldn't go out of the house. That's what happened to Big Sandy and Sir Robert![15]

Donald's Purse

There was a lad from Stonybridge in Uist called Donald Smith working at Tirinie along with me. We were great friends. One day we got our wages at midday at the term and we got the rest of the day off and went down to the town. Well, we had things to pay for that we had had from the merchants on credit until the term day. The first thing I did when we came into the town was to go and pay my debts, every penny that I owed. I sent some money home and kept a little for myself. I was engaged to stay and go on working where I was.

I asked Donald Smith if he had got clear of the merchants. 'No,' he said, 'I didn't go near them.'

'Well, it's time you did,' I said.

'Och, there's such a crush there, I'll let them be tonight. We'll come along on Saturday evening. We'll have a better chance then.'

'All right,' I said.

We went down to the station. A farmer who lived two miles nearer Aberfeldy than we did, met us at the station. We ourselves were four miles away from the town. He asked if we would be going soon. We said we would.

'If you're going right away,' he said, 'my cart is here, you'll get a lift in it as far as I'm going.'

Oh, that was fine. We asked him if he would come for a dram. Yes, he would. We went into the Station Hotel. There were tap-rooms there, and we went into one of them, and Donald went and got the dram. We didn't sit down at all, we went out right away.

'Off you go then,' he said, 'along to the Square and see if you see my maid, she's here along with me. I'm going to harness.'

All right. We went along to the Square. The maid was the daughter of a woman who lived up near ourselves, who used to work all autumn at harvest work on the farm where I was, called Mistress Ian Dick. She had two daughters. This one, Mary, was working on farms, and the other one was dressmaking at home. We went along; the girl met us at the Square, and told us that her master was coming with the cart. We just stood where we were until he came. The girl and I went into the box of the cart. Donald went and jumped on the trams on the other side of the cart (from the farmer). He and the farmer were talking all the way until we reached the place where the farm road joined the main road. We jumped off the cart then. The farmer was going down to his own farm, to his own place beside the river Tay.

We went home. When Donald was getting undressed he put his hand in his pocket. There was no sign of his purse, which had all his wages for six months in it. He nearly went crazy. I was as upset as he was. I couldn't give him much help at all, I had run out myself, my purse was empty enough. Donald would have to lift the wages he hadn't yet earned or else he wouldn't keep up his credit. He had neither credit nor money now.

But on Saturday evening a little boy of the farmer's came in, he was only just going to school, he was only six years old.

'Mistress Dick was wanting you, Angus, to go down tonight, she has some business with you.'

Well, I thought that the other fellows had asked him to say that, when they had heard that her daughter had been coming from Aberfeldy in the cart along with me.

'Who asked you to say that?' I said.

'Mistress Dick,' he said.

'I'll give you Mistress Dick,' I said, 'if you don't get out of my sight.' He went out and didn't say a word.

The next Saturday the eldest of Mr Menzies' sons[16] came in. This one was fifteen years old, he was in the High School. The little boy was along with him.

'Mistress Dick is wanting you, Angus, to go down tonight,

to remember to go down tonight, she's got some business with you.'

'What business has Mistress Dick got with me?'

'Oh, heavens, I don't know,' he said. 'Didn't Ralf bring you word a week ago tonight?'

'He did,' I said.

'Well, she's insisting we didn't tell you at all,' he said. 'She was threatening to take the breeks off us.'

Oh, a great big powerful woman, she weighed eighteen stone and was as strong as a horse; a terrible Amazon! I remember myself, when she was forking hay, and the fork she had belonged to one of the men. He was wanting it from her and she wouldn't give it to him. Well, he caught hold of it to take it from her and another of the lads jumped in along with him to help him. She only had hold of the end of the fork—and the two of them couldn't take it from her. At last she turned on them and said, 'If you make me let go of it, I'll take your breeks off you unless you clear off.' They fled and left her there, herself and the fork!

Never mind, here I was looking at Donald; and I asked:

'Goodness, what does Mistress Ian Dick want to see me about?'

'What could she want to see you about, unless she's heard you were coming home with her daughter the night of the term?'

'Weren't you coming home with her daughter yourself just as much as I was?'

'Oh, it was you that was in the cart along with her.'

'You were in the cart too. It's not likely that's what she wants to see me about, whatever it is.'

'What is it, then?' he said.

'Heavens, I don't know.'

'Oh, nothing else but that.'

'Tut, keep quiet. It's likely they're cracked.'

'They're all cracked,' he said.

'Get ready,' I said, 'and we'll go down when I've come out of the stable.'

'Devil a step.'

'Tut! What harm will it do to you? It's not right not to go after the message coming twice. Won't you go then?'

Not a bit. My word, unwilling as I was, I didn't like to stay. I went. When I arrived, there was a bright light from each end of the house. I knocked at the door. Who came to the door but Mary, the daughter who was working for the farmer! I was certainly surprised that she was in at this time of the night. Then she asked me so kindly to come in. 'Come in, come in; sit down, sit down.' I went in. Mistress Dick was sitting in a big chair beside the fire. I took hold of a little stool that was there to sit on. She got up. 'You shan't sit there at all, you shan't sit there at all. Sit down here.'

'A wise man never sat down in the place of the mistress of the house,' I said.

'You'll sit down there. You'll sit where I ask you to!'

I went and sat down on the chair. The girl turned and put the kettle on the fire at once. Mistress Dick got up and went across the room, kicking aside everything she encountered, making every pail she met ring. She looked at me. I had no idea in the world what she was meaning. I was saying to myself that it must be something accursed I had been falsely accused of. Then she went and shut the door and stood with her back to it.

'Didn't Mr Menzies' children bring you word to come down here a week ago tonight?'

'Well, yes,' I said, 'but sometimes they're hard to believe.'

'I'm sure they are, and so are other people,' she said. 'But what the devil were you doing to my daughter the night of the term?'

I didn't know what on earth to say, with the girl opposite me!

'What could I do to her but what I'd do to her mother?'

'You rascal, you won't get out of it so easily as that. That answer won't do when I've sent for you. But it's as well for you you came tonight or else I'd have sent someone to fetch you who'd have made you come.'

'Upon my soul, mother,' said the girl, 'keep quiet, you'll make the young man take to his heels.'

'Upon my word, he can't run away,' said Mistress Dick, with her back to the door.

'Well, indeed, it isn't very easy to do it just now,' I said.

49

'Amn't I put to a loss on your account! There she is now, sent home! What are you going to do now? You must take her and keep her!'

I heard the girl who was down in the bedroom end of the house burst into laughter that could have been heard outside! By God, I said to myself, she was just trying to take a rise out of me!

'Take it easy,' I said, 'I don't know but that's something I'd be pretty well pleased about.'

'Oh, well, well, well, right enough,' she said, 'if that's so, we'll be more friendly to you.'

'Well, indeed, so you should,' I said.

She lifted a chair to sit beside me. I'd as soon have had the Evil Spirit sitting there!

'Mr Menzies up there wants nothing more than married farm-servants who'll stay with him, he's plenty of cottages there with no one in them; it's likely enough I'll be getting my dinner with you when I'm working up there.'

'It's likely you will and your supper too,' I said.

'Oh, well then, it looks as if the business is all right. And when are you going to marry her?'

'Oh, I'm sure I must wait until the next term,' I said.

'That won't do, but at once! What's she going to be doing here? There's another one here! And you must be married by the minister and turn with her!'

'By the Book, I'll turn, but it'll be in bed!'

'That won't do!'

'What'll I do now?'

The girl near by was keeping on asking her to be quiet, but she only got worse.

'Well, I don't mind, if she's willing herself. Aren't we all seeking towards the same God?'

'Yes, indeed,' I said.

'Well, then, you won't delay. Your name will be on the board tomorrow!'

I didn't know what in the world to say to her. I was saying to myself, 'You wicked girl, if this was your business with me, you deserved to be boiled, that's what you deserved.'[17]

The girl had tea ready and she called to her sister to come to the kitchen, and she came in then, with something in her hand.

'My word,' she said, 'didn't you get the dressing-down!'

'That I did,' I said, 'if every man received the like, they wouldn't be going with the girls so often.'

'Indeed they wouldn't,' she said.

'Oh, the rascal,' said Mistress Dick, 'my word, the young fellow isn't so easy to confound.'

'Well, so he needs to be,' I said.

'Come on, come on now, take your tea; come on! We'll have many a tea together yet!'

'I hope we will. Things are only dry tonight, but——'

'It'll be better than this yet! Come on! Take your tea!'

When tea was over the girl got up.

'Heavens,' she said, 'it's time for me to go or I'll be locked out. Did you lose anything the night of the term, Angus?'

I thought of Donald's purse. My goodness!

'Well, I didn't lose anything, but my friend did, and it's the same as if I had lost it myself.'

'What did he lose?' she said.

'His purse and his pay,' I said.

'Well, I found it.'

'Where on earth did you find it?'

'I found it in the box of the cart. When I was getting out of the cart down at the farm, it was just beneath my feet. When I went into the light, I saw what it was. I asked him himself if he had lost anything, and he said he had not. He was asking what I had found but he didn't find that out; and I thought it was you who had lost it, it was you who were sitting in the cart.'

'Well, it wasn't me who lost it at all,' I said.

'It slipped out of his pocket when he was sitting at the front of the cart,' she said.

'Yes, that's what it did,' I said. 'The trousers he was wearing, nothing at all would stay in their pockets; they had side pockets.'

'Well then,' she said, 'you take it to him.'

'I certainly will,' I said.

Indeed, I was very happy when I heard that this was the

business she had with me! I went and opened it and took out a pound.

'Well, I'll venture to give one of them to you for your honesty.'

She wouldn't take a ha'penny.

'She won't take it,' said her mother, 'you take it to the poor fellow who it belongs to. He worked for it hard enough.'

'Well, if she won't take it, I hope he'll remember it some other way; if he forgets, he isn't worth much.'

'My word, then, you aren't going to get off with that.'

'I'm not asking to get off,' I said.

'Well, now you must go and see her safe home, after coming up here tonight and a week ago tonight, to see you.'

'By the Book, I'll see her home though it were to London.'

'Take good care, then, you don't do anything wrong to her.'

'I won't, indeed.'

I went with the daughter of Mistress Ian Dick until I had left her in the kitchen. The people in the house had gone to bed when we arrived, but the door was only bolted on the outside and the lamp had been left alight in the kitchen. I made for home then. Everyone was asleep. I went in, and I went up the stairs, and I prodded Donald. He raised his head.

'You've come!'

'Yes.'

'What business did that damned old wife have with you?'

'It was for the girl,' I said.

'That damned girl!' he said. I began to laugh.

'Lift your head,' I said. 'Look at that!'

'What's that?'

'Look at your purse!'

He jumped up out of the bed with nothing on. I'm sure that no money ever gave him greater pleasure.

'But who found this?' he said.

'Ian Dick's Mary,' I said.

'Where on earth did she find it?'

'In the box of the cart. That's what you're thinking you lost in Aberfeldy.'

'Amn't I lucky! If you hadn't been courting Ian Dick's daughter I'd never have got a penny of it!'

'Here's every penny of it,' I said. 'But see and remember to give her something for her honesty. I offered her a pound, and she wouldn't take a ha'-penny from me.'

'By the Book, she'll get that.' He was as happy as a king. And that's how I left Mistress Ian Dick!

The Best Games I Ever Saw

(The next autumn, Angus and Donald Smith took Mary Dick to the Highland Games at Birnam in return for finding Donald's purse.)

We used to go to the Aberfeldy games, every one of us. One year we were at the Aberfeldy games and there was nothing there but what we were familiar enough with, dancing and piping and races. But the next year there were games advertised, to be at Birnam. Cavalry were to be there, and the Seaforth Highlanders; there was to be a sham fight. This was worth going to see. There was to be cheap fares, we would get a return ticket for less than we'd pay for a single before that, from every station in Scotland.

Anyway, the Aberfeldy games were to be in the summer, and the Birnam games in the autumn. We all agreed together that none of us would go to the Aberfeldy games. We were at work thinning turnips. Anyway, one evening the boss came along to where we were.

'Well, indeed,' he said. 'I didn't know my lads were so wise. You didn't go to the Aberfeldy games.'

'We didn't,' we said. 'We've been there before.'

'Oh, it's a good thing you found that out,' he said; 'going there wouldn't put a penny in your pockets, whatever it would take out.'

But anyway when the day of the Birnam games was going to come off, it was a very good autumn, and there was a twenty-acre field of oats ready to put in. We asked the grieve to speak to the boss himself and say that we expected to go to the games. He wouldn't. 'Speak to him yourselves.' On the morning of the day of the games all we did when we had fed and cleaned the horses in the stables was to go to the bothy and start putting on our (good) clothes. When the boss was getting

53

tired waiting for us to come out he went to the stable. There was no one there but the grieve.

'Where are the lads?' he said.

'I don't know,' said the grieve, 'they're over there in the bothy.'

'What are they doing there?'

'Going to the games.'

'Going to the games?' He went over to the bothy. I was downstairs washing my face, and the others were upstairs getting dressed.

'What's this?' the boss said, standing in the doorway. 'Where are the others?'

'Upstairs,' I said.

'What are they doing there?'

'Getting dressed to go to the games.'

'To go to the games?' All Scotland wouldn't do for you! Well, well, well, I never heard the like. If it rains after today it won't be forgotten for five years!' He looked at his watch. 'Very well, you'll have to get a move on if you're going to catch the train. When you're ready, come down to the house, I'm sure you'll need money. Duncan[18] will take down those of you that are ready, they'll go in a minute. When the other meet him, he'll return with them, so you won't lose the train the machine won't take you all together.'

Oh, how pleased we were! We went off. We had to change trains at Ballinluig. We got out at Ballinluig. Three trains went through the station and not a single person could get a seat in them; the people in the station were crushing each other to death! The stationmaster was keeping them back, telling them to, 'Take it easy, you'll get a train presently.'

Anyway, we got away on the fourth train, and when we arrived, before we went into the games at all, we came upon two girls there who were engaged in dancing on a stage. They had a little terrier, a lapdog, and they were wearing short knee-length dresses, and they were wearing boots and hard hats like you used to see coachmen wearing. The dog was as good at dancing as they were, cutting capers on the platform. Then a hat would fall off and as they came around, the hat would be kicked up and would land on one of their heads on the way down!

But for pity's sake, up went the dog then beneath one of the dresses. I could see no sign of it; then I saw it put its head out at the girl's neck; it withdrew its head. In a moment, I saw a bulge come on the sleeve of her jacket, and the dog put out its head at her hand! It withdrew it. The girls were dancing and the crowd was gathering. We were then asked to go into a hall they had there. When we went in we sat down on benches there. One of the girls went up on the stage. She had a table on the stage. She went over with two jam jars and turned them on their sides on the table so we might see there was nothing in them. There was a box full of sawdust beneath the table. She filled one of the jars with sawdust. She put three handfuls in the jar and put a card on its mouth.

Then she took a handkerchief—the kind I've often seen belonging to tramps—a red speckled one, and folded it, and put it in the other jar and put a card on' its mouth. Then she took a pistol and put a threepenny bit in a piece of paper and began twisting it until she made a narrow neck so long on it. She held it out and fired at it with the revolver, and off went the threepenny bit. She went and lifted the card off the jar where she'd put the sawdust, and a dove hopped out of it on to the table, and shook itself, and a cloud of sawdust came off its feathers. It hopped on to her shoulder and hopped off her shoulder over to the window. It was cooing and walking backwards and forwards in the window. I was watching it, and I would swear that it was one of the pigeons that are at Loch Eynort!

Then the girl lifted the card from the other jar and a snake so long came out of it, down on to the table, and oh! she met it with the jar at the end of the table and it went back into the jar. She put a card on the mouth of the jar. I said to myself I had been long enough in this accursed place! So Donald Smith and I made off for the games inside.

And they were the best games I have ever been at! They began with the cavalry, with a sham fight. The horses first of all were jumping over a height. There were four hurdles set before them. Tops of trees had been put on them, so that they would not hurt the feet of the horses jumping over them. The horse that jumped highest was to get a prize. When that was over, then four posts were put up in the middle of the field. There was a plank of wood across the top of each post, and there was a piece of wire on the outside end of the plank with a lemon put on it. Then they came with the horses to see who could cut the four lemons with a sword, just going past at full gallop. Well, one of them got the four!

When they had finished with that, the lemons were replaced with rings, and then they got lances, to see who could take the four rings. Some of them managed it. None of them missed entirely. Then pegs were driven into the earth with mallets. Then they got lances and the horses came one after another at full gallop to see who could take away the pegs. Well, there were (only) three or four who didn't have a peg on their lance points coming round and going back. That's something as neat as I ever saw horses doing.

Next there were three poles set up on each side, and a ball was put on the top of each pole. The poles were not in line at all. Then they came with the horses with narrow poles in their hands to see if they could knock the balls off the top of the poles with the pole in their hands. Well, it was seldom they failed; no one was missing entirely, no one.

When this was over, they gathered together and went out through the gate in fours behind the wood all of them. Then the Seaforth Highlanders came. They made a camp at the top end of the field. Then an officer came with a soldier and set him on guard there. They were acting Zulus, and wearing soft hats. Where did they put him on guard but at one of the hurdles the horses had been jumping over. He was going back and forth there. The officer went back. The camp became quiet. There was no one to be seen except the man who was on guard. Then he went and knocked down a hurdle and was looking up now and again, and didn't see anything. Then he would look at the outer gate, and he wasn't seeing anything. Then he went and sat on the hurdle. He next put his hand under his arm and took out a bottle, and took a drink from the bottle. It wasn't long before he began to fall asleep, and at last he was fast asleep.

Then two scouts, two of the horsemen, came in towards the gate. When they saw the guard asleep, oh! they turned around back. In three minutes they were in at the gate, in fours just at the gate. Well, these two scouts came in and went around clear of the guard, and one of them dismounted and caught hold of his rifle and bent his knee and was going to shoot him. But he didn't like to kill him asleep. He began to creep up on him until he reached him, and when he reached him, he took a look, and first of all he took the rifle and bayonet away from him. Then he looked and saw the bottle; he caught hold of the bottle and lifted it up to the sun to see if he could get a dram out of it; he put it into his breast pocket. He got a piece of rope and tied the guard's two feet together, and when he had tied his feet together, he took him by the neck, and gave him his fists around his head! Oh, the guard let out yells asking for mercy, mercy, mercy! The scout then went and took hold of the end of the rope and took the guard over to the other scout, a prisoner.

He held out the rope to the other man, and the guard—his stride was no longer than a hen's with his two feet practically nailed together! However, he was looking now and again at the scout who had taken him, who was behind him, and when he saw the scout putting his foot on the stirrup to mount his horse, he jerked the rope when he was on the horse's back, and off he went! The scout gave a yell and the other man jumped out of the saddle and caught hold of his rifle and fired it after him and he fell dead on the ground with a bullet in his back, and lay flat there.

But dear me, this woke the people in the camp. What confusion there was getting ready! In went the horses then, and they were just like shadows coming in at the gate, every four, they were just going in a single file the other way. Then there came a volley down from the garrison, and the foremost horse fell. The other horses fell like a wave, flat on the ground. The soldiers jumped behind them. The rifles were aimed over the horses' bodies and the firing began; you saw nothing then but smoke, with blanks.

The horse in front that had fallen had broken its legs. The soldier began to bandage the small of its leg. A man in the camp noticed him and rushed down to bayonet him, and he himself was hit and fell; but he managed to drag himself back into the camp. The other man bandaged the horse's leg; it was its hind leg that had been broken. But the cavalry were firing two bullets to every one the men in the camp were firing. Then they got the order to charge. They jumped on to their horses' backs and the man whose horse's leg had been broken, jumped up behind another man. Up they went then and the noise the horses made going up, my dear fellow, would have frightened you. In they went amongst them. A horse got up on his hind legs and went the length of a house on them, with the soldier on his back, whinnying, because he wasn't just being allowed to trample them with his feet. They took the camp. Everything was quiet after that and there was nothing to be seen but the man who had been on guard, who was dead in the middle of the field, and the horse that had broken its leg, it was stretched out over on the other side.

But what was more wonderful than that the man who was dead lifted his head and looked up towards the camp, and wasn't seeing anything. Then he noticed the horse. He crept a bit on all fours, stopping now and again, no one knew where he was going, but he was making straight for the dead horse. Then he reached the horse and went up to its body. He was a while there, then he saw its leg was bandaged. He began to try its leg to see where it was broken. Then he began to untie the bandage. He untied the bandage. Then he made out that its leg was not broken at all. Next he went and untied the horse's head. He lifted its head and let go of it, and it fell with a thud on the ground! Then he went and began to open the horses eyes and to look in them. The horse didn't move, didn't budge. Then he caught hold of its mouth and began to blow into the horse's mouth, and oh! how everyone laughed when they saw him putting breath into the horse! Then he let go of its head and let its head down. Then he lifted its head a little. Then he began to make his way over the ground until he put his foot on the saddle, across its back. The horse jumped on its feet and off it went, making for the gate. The man on its back lifted his hat to cheer the men who were sitting! The people in the camp noticed him. Two others went after him

—just as if you saw a rabbit running before a dog! When the two horses were up to him he was throwing himself on the ground; the other two were going past him. He would take the other way.

At last, one of them got in front of him, and the other was behind him just at the time they were coming around; the first horseman's sword was raised. He held up his hands, the horse bent its head between its legs. You never saw the like of that horse there, staggering along after having been captured, with a soldier on each side of him! Well, that was the best thing I ever saw, to be watching them!

We came home and the next day we began putting in the corn, and we didn't keep account of the time until the last sheaf[19] was in the stack-yard, working until it got dark. The boss got in every bit of corn dry enough, although there were other people's crops, and plenty of them, rotting on the fields; and he himself was saying he hadn't lost by letting the lads go to the games, his harvest was in the stack-yard, while other farmers' crops were rotting today on the fields!

4

BORENICH

WHEN I left Tirinie, I told my master I was going home, that I wasn't going to engage at all. Well, that was all right with him, when he heard that it was home I was going to. 'That's a good thing,' he said, 'a lad wanting to keep his home up.'

Then I went to Aberfeldy, to the hiring fair. There was a lad from Uist out there, and he met me in the town, and asked me if I had been hired. 'I've not,' I said, 'I haven't been hired yet.'

'Do you want a place?' he said.

'I do,' I said.

'Well,' he said, 'a man was speaking to me down there just now, to see if I could get a secondman for him.'

'Where's he at?' I asked.

'Beside Loch Tummel.'

'Is it a good place?'

'It is, indeed,' he said. 'I spent three years working for him.'

Well, you could only get a year's engagement, engagements of six months weren't going at all.

'Oh, well, if you spent three years there,' I said, 'I think I might spend one. Is he a good master?'

'Oh, yes, indeed. Come along, then, I've only just left the boss here.'

We went along; the farmer met us just at the square.

'Here's a lad for you,' said the Uistman, 'who hasn't found a place yet.'

'Oh, very good,' said the farmer—Thomas MacDonald was his name—'very good. Are you working here already?'

'I am,' I said. 'I'm working at Tirinie.'

'Oh, aye. Is it there you are?'

'It is,' I said.

'How long is it since you came there?'

'It's more than two years,' I said.

'Oh, indeed then, it's likely you'd be fit enough for me. It's a secondman I'm needing. What wages do you want?'

'I'd need to get sixteen pounds or fifteen pounds anyway,'[1] I said.

'Ah, well,' he said, 'wages are down this year. No one's getting more than fifteen pounds. But I'll give you thirteen.'

'Oh, that won't do,' I said.

'Oh, well, there isn't so much work to do for me as there is at Tirinie at all. I know Tirinie very well.'

'Well, I'm sure it isn't to be taking my ease that you want me for. How many acres have you in every break?'

'About twenty.'

'And you've only two pairs of horses?'

'Yes.'

'Well, I'm sure there'll be plenty of work there itself.'

There was a young lad standing on the pavement, on the edge of the pavement, just a little beyond us, craning himself to listen to us. He now came over behind me and caught hold of my arm and squeezed it.

'Ah, Thomas,' he said, 'this lad is too soft in the bone for you!'

Thomas turned on him angrily. 'You let him alone, soft or hard in the bone though he be, until I'm finished with him,' he said. The other fellow only passed on laughing and stood a little beyond us.

'Well,' said Thomas, 'you'll get fourteen pounds, then, and your lodging free above that.'

'Oh, very good,' I said.

He went and put his hand in his pocket then and gave me a crown as airles money. Then he went to see Robert Menzies, my boss.

'I've just engaged one of your lads,' he said to him.

'Oh, have you?' said Robert. 'Which one of them have you got?'

'Angus MacLellan.'

'Aye? I didn't think that fellow was going to engage today at all.'

'Well, I've engaged him for a year,' said Thomas. 'Is he a steady lad?'

'Well, if you're asking for his reference,' said Robert, 'if I'd known that he was engaging today, neither you nor anyone else would have got him if he could have been kept where he is.'

No doubt Thomas was pleased then! The next day, Robert Menzies came where I was working.

'So,' he said, 'did you engage at the fair?'

'Well, I did, but I didn't expect to at all when I left the house.'

'Well, then,' he said, 'it's best for you to stay where you are, and I'll send him—what did he give you as airles money?'

'He gave me a crown.'

'I'll send it to him myself, then, if you'll stay where you are.'

'Do you want to send me to prison?' I asked.

'He won't do anything to you if you stay where you are,' he said. 'But if you engaged elsewhere, he could go for you.'

'How would you like it yourself?' I said. 'Indeed, however bad he is, I'll spend a year there, anyway.'

'I'm sure you will. Ah, well, then, see you don't engage at Pitlochry fair next year until I've seen you there.'

'Indeed I won't.'

I spent a year working for poor Thomas, and he was a good master. We ate at the same table with him all the year, every one of us, and he never let us go out on a bad day; we had to stay inside with the horses; we'd get something to do.

Next year I wanted to come home that winter, after the New Year; my brother Hector had been sailing, and had died in France; only my father and mother were at home, and I said to myself that it would be very sad for them to be alone all the winter, and that I'd go home to be with them for a while. On the day of Pitlochry fair, I didn't go there at all; I was afraid that if I did go, I would be snapped up by somebody. I stayed thatching stacks all day! When Thomas came home at nightfall, he said:

'You didn't go to the hiring fair at all.'

'I didn't.'

'Well, I saw your master, your old master,' he said, 'and he was asking for you; but I told him you were going home for the winter, and that you weren't going to engage at all.'

That's how I left Tirinie and went to Borenich.

It was in November that I left. There was only one hiring fair in the year, just a fortnight before the November term. A great many used to collect there; there would be hundreds at it. The town would be just thick with them at that time. There is nothing like it at all today. There was a hiring fair at Perth, the biggest hiring fair in Scotland, Littledennan Market it was called. There was a hiring fair in every town. There was one in Stirling, and one in Perth, and one in Inverness. They were everywhere. Another place where they used to engage, was at the barracks, when they were in the Militia, the day the Militia broke up. Every farmer who needed a lad, was going there. That's where I engaged first, and I ran away!

You had to stay for a year. It was most often for a year, but throughout Argyll it was for six months, pretty often. It was long enough if a man happened to go to a bad place. If he happened to go to a good one, he needn't mind though he'd engaged for two years. There were bad enough places in some parts. I knew a lad who was on a farm beside us, when I was at Borenich, a farm two miles down the loch from us, called Bail' an t-Seilich. The farm-servants weren't staying, plenty of them were leaving at half-term. The farmer had only one farm-servant; he himself used to be out working along with him. I understand that the farmer was not so bad at all, but his wife was much worse than he was himself. He and his wife weren't getting on with the farm-servants at all. The farm-servants wouldn't let her inside the bothy door, she must stay in her own place. The farm-servant was doing everything in the bothy.

On term day, what was he at but the threshing. It was a horse-mill, and he was driving the horses outside, and the master was inside feeding the mill. The farm-servant had his watch in his hand, and when it was twelve o'clock, he shouted 'whoa' to the horses and left them standing in the mill. He went into the bothy. He had only just gone into the bothy, when the farmer's wife came in after him and told him to get out.

'This is my place now,' she said, 'clear out of here.'

He looked. He had a pail of water he had brought in to wash himself. He threw the pailful of water over her head. 'You get out now,' he said. 'I'll be ready before you're dry!'

She just turned and went out. The farmer came. He didn't say a word but let the horses out of the mill and went in and came out with the farm-servant's wages and handed them to him!

The Night the Cow Calved

Tommy MacDonald had a cattleman, an Irishman who had been with him for sixteen years. This year he had fallen ill with rheumatism and taken to his bed. Tommy's sisters were looking after the cattle with the help of the maid there. I and the other man didn't have anything to do with them, except that we went to give help at times. The boss was travelling all over the place, only spending an occasional night at home.

This night I went over to the cowshed to help the women give the cattle their evening feed. There was a cow in calf there, at the point of calving; she was overdue. The boss's sister Mary said to me:

'Do you know anything about cattle, Angus?'

'Oh, I can tell them apart from horses,' I said.

'Look at that cow, is it long until she'll calve?' (A black hornless cow.)

'I don't think it'll be long before she calves,' I said.

'Her time is up,' she said. 'It looks like we'll have to stay up tonight.'

'What will you give me if I stay up for you?'

'Anything you like.'

'Oh, off with you then'—the maid was a Skye girl—'off with you, to bed. I'll stay.' I knew perfectly well the cow wouldn't calve!

They went to bed. I went to the bothy. I thought I would go out to the cowshed before I went to bed. I lit a lantern and looked in. Every single beast in the cowshed was lying down.

I heard the noise of footsteps over from the other side of the close, at the stable door. I stopped to see what it was. A big lump of a tramp appeared, a big red-headed man, looking for shelter. It was a calm frosty night.

The women had made a pen ready for the calf and had put straw in it. I thought it would be a good place for to let the tramp into. 'Come here, then,' I said, 'there's a place for you, stretch yourself out there, but see you get up early and clear out before anyone else comes, before they get up, so they don't find out that I let you in.' I got sacks for him to cover himself with. Oh, he was royally off there!

We got up at five o'clock, that was the time we used to rise there anyway, and we came out. Who did we see in the close but the boss's sister and the maid, going to the cowshed to do the milking.

'Has the cow calved, Angus?' she said.

'Yes.'

'Goodness, why didn't you wake us?'

'Oh, I didn't need to wake you.'

'What kind of calf has she got?'

'A big red bull-calf. It's in the pen over there, see and give it something.'

She went over with a lantern. The tramp was asleep, with the sacks over his head. She began to lift the sacks. Then his head appeared. 'Oh, your darling bare red head!' she said. The tramp turned his two eyes on her. She let out a yell and fell in the door of the pen! The other lad ran over to see what was wrong.

'What's wrong?' he said.

'Never mind what's wrong. He's got the devil in the pen!'

The poor Irishman got up—he was an Irishman, too—and started to put on his clothes. I went over to the stable. Dear me, the mouth she made, because of the trick that had been played on her! I didn't say anything. When I came in for my breakfast, she was standing on the other side of the room watching me steadily.

'Did you give the calf something?' I said, turning to her.

She broke into laughter. 'Oh, though you were to go to the scaffold, you'd get off!'

It was some calf she had! The boss was told about it, and nearly burst himself laughing. 'Oh, he did for you all right!' he said. 'He just did for you all right!'

A Sore Neck

Once I caught cold at the threshing. There was frost and snow all winter; it came a little after Christmas and didn't go until the middle of spring; it went away with the most beautiful weather. Well, I was at the threshing this day. The threshing mill was driven by water, and the water for the mill came from a loch that was a long way away on top of the hill. I was sweating working indoors at the mill, and I had to go to turn off the water; and I didn't take my jacket or anything with me, I just went in my shirt sleeves. Before I got back, my shirt had frozen as hard as an oilskin, and I was shivering with cold.

Well, no doubt we had a good bothy, with a fire on for us every night. The next day when I got up I was all right, except that my neck was a little sore. I thought that my head having been too high up was the reason it was sore. The next day, it wasn't the least better; it was getting worse all the time. I didn't use to wear anything round my neck. I went and put a scarf around it then. My word, then it got terribly sore, and I wasn't sleeping at all on account of it. This day, when we were home in the evening, our supper was on the table. When I saw it on the table, though it was near enough to me, I only sat on a chair aside, while the others sat down at the table. The farmer's sister looked at me:

'Aren't you going to take your supper at all?' she said.

'Not tonight,' I said.

'What's wrong with you?'

'Oh, nothing.'

'Well,' she said, 'is there something wrong with your neck? What's round your neck there?'

'My neck's sore,' I said.

She came over and took the scarf off my neck, and looked at it.

'When did you feel this?' she said.

'It's a week since I first felt it.'

'Indeed,' she said, 'you poor wretch, a week, and you've been out every day like that.'

'I have,' I said.

'Would you have gone out if you'd been with your father and mother?'

'Well, I'm sure I wouldn't.'

'Poor wretch,' she said, 'that's what you are.'

She went off then, saying, 'you must try to take something.'

'Oh, I won't take anything tonight.'

'You'll take something, you must. You won't manage like that. You'll take a little semolina,' she said.

'All right, a very little.'

Every time I swallowed anything it felt like a thorn going into my neck.

Next day she said to her brother Thomas:

'You'd better go to the doctor for Angus. He isn't at all well.'

'I'm going to the town today,' he said. 'I'll see the doctor.'

He went there; he told the doctor I was bad with a sore neck. The doctor gave him a line to the chemist for iodine and said it should be painted twice a day with it, with iodine, and that that would stop it. Thomas returned with that, and his sister began to paint it, but great God! if it was bad before, it was bad then! At last I had to stay in bed. I just couldn't bear her coming near me then! I was going out of my mind. My neck swelled up, and it was all I could do to get my breath, I was nearly choked by it! That night in the bothy I got the bed to myself. There was an Irishman and another fellow, a blacksmith's son, and another shepherd who was wintering wethers, along with me. I was seeing every possible kind of person, dead and alive; I was seeing my father and mother beside me, and I was talking to them. When the others went into their breakfast in the morning, the farmer's sister asked how I was.

'I think he's only very middling,' said the smith's son. 'We didn't get much sleep since night came, owing to him talking, and we couldn't make out a single word of what he was saying.'

'Ah, well,' she said, 'that's all that needs to be said about it.'

67

She went out. I couldn't lie down, I was just sitting against the pillow at the head of the bed.

'You're bad today all right,' she said.

'I am, indeed.'

'Oh, this won't do,' she said, 'we must fetch the doctor.'

Thomas himself came in then.

'Oh,' he said. He had a nephew who was a medical student who was on holiday staying at the inn up the road from us, at the Tummel Inn. 'I'll go to get my nephew, and he'll come to see you.'

He went off. He didn't have far to go. The nephew came, a young fellow who had plenty of Gaelic; a nice chap. He looked at it.

'Ah,' he said, 'it's time it was lanced. That's the thing, it must be lanced.'

'Will you lance it yourself?' said Thomas.

'Oh, I can't do that yet,' he said. 'But send for the doctor, and I'll come along with him.'

The doctor was living in Pitlochry, nine miles away.

'All right,' said Thomas. 'I'd better send him a telegram, and you take it along to the post office.'

'I will.'

He took the telegram and went off. A reply came that the doctor would be here at ten o'clock tomorrow morning. That night I didn't get a wink of sleep; I was only just able to breathe. The doctor came at ten o'clock, and Thomas's nephew with him; they came in. I could smell the whisky off him as soon as he opened the door; he was very heavy on the drink. Dr Robertson was his name; he was a Gael too.

'What's wrong with you, my lad?' he said.

He came over to the bed. 'Oh, well,' he said, 'we must take him out of bed. This won't do.'

My trousers were put on me and I was taken out of the bed and put to sit on a chair beside the window. The doctor examined me. 'Have you any whisky?' he said, turning to the farmer's sister.

'We have,' she said, 'and wine.'

'Go and bring some.'

She went and came back with a bottle. The doctor took out the cork and poured some into a tumbler.

'Here,' he said, 'try to swallow this.'

'Oh, I'm afraid I can't manage it,' I said.

'Go on! Och! You're no Highlander if you can't drink that!'

I tried it in my mouth, and it nearly choked me, it came out through my nose. 'Poor fellow, you're very bad. But take it easy, you'll be better presently.' He took a lump of cotton out of his bag, and put it on my shoulder, and said to the student, 'Look behind him and catch hold of his arms.'

'He doesn't need to,' I said, 'I'll hold my arms myself.'

I was afraid that if he took my arm behind me, the side of my neck would tear, it was so hard.

'Oh, very good, very good,' said the doctor, 'you weren't brought up in this district. There's some around here, if a thorn goes into their little finger, they'll need chloroform before it's removed. See you don't move now.'

'I'll not move.'

My God, when he put the lance in, I felt—Mary Mother, the noise it made, I thought there were teeth in it, with the noise it made going through. But then came the worst smell I had ever smelt. I saw the doctor himself turn his head. Then he put his hand on it to squeeze it, and when he did that, he sent me into a faint, and I just went out, and became unconscious. When I opened my eyes, the farmer's sister was there with a dish of cold water, and the doctor was putting water on my hands.

'How are you, lad?' he said, turning to me.

'I'm better,' I said. I answered right off.

'Oh, very good, very good. We won't trouble you any more today. He's suffered too much,' he said. 'It should have been lanced three days ago. But we'll leave it alone today. I'll leave stuff here to be put on it, until I come tomorrow.'

Then he gave her a box of ointment. He got lint, and cut it into square pieces, and bandaged it. 'Now, you put a fresh one of these on every three hours, until I come tomorrow. You'll have to sit up with him.'

'I'll do that,' she said. 'Anything you ask.'

'Where's the bottle now?' he said. 'I'll bet he'll take it now.'

He got the bottle, and my word, he took a dram of it himself! I took half a glass of it then, and it went down! I thought I was a good deal stronger.

The farmer's sister was sitting on a chair beside my bed all night; the servant-girl was willing to take her place there, for her to get some sleep; she wouldn't do that at all. 'I'm not going to risk him to anyone but myself. You go to bed; you might fall asleep yourself.' When the doctor came at ten o'clock next day, he took out a probe with a lump at its end, and put it into the wound, and began to prod it, and squeeze it, and my God! that was the worst pain I felt of all; until at last there was a stream of red blood running down my shoulder. Then he bandaged it up. 'Well,' he said, 'it'll be all right from now on. But you put one of these plasters on it twice a day, and every time you put it on, keep the wound open in case it heals outside more quickly than it heals inside. If it does that, it could start all over again. I'll call whenever I'm passing.'

The farmer's sister looked after me, and my word, she was a good nurse. Every morning she came in with a glass of wine for me, before I got my breakfast.

One day the doctor called when he was passing. By then I had got up to sit at table along with them. Oh, the doctor was pleased, he came up and stripped the bandage off, and looked at it, and praised the job she had made of it, it was getting on so well. It was healing very well; I was working while it was open. 'It's healing very well,' he said. 'That's the place we find most difficult to lance, a person's neck or a woman's breast. There's nothing there but veins and sinews, and it's very difficult to avoid them when there's a swelling there. You needn't be dressing it more than once a day now.'

I never felt anything from it any more after that; but indeed I was telling myself it was a good thing I was where I was, that if it had happened to me at Tirinie I would never have got up again.

As for the lancing, I only felt the one stab, but when the doctor began to squeeze it, it was then I felt the pain!

The Irishmen and the Posts

The Irishman who worked at Borenich along with me as cattleman and the other farm-servant along with me there were always at odds with each other. There was no day but they were quarrelling about something. The Irishman was praising Ireland, saying how good they were at working, Scotland couldn't manage if the Irishmen weren't there. The other fellow was dead against him, contradicting him.

We used to sleep in a bothy, and take our food indoors along with the farmer himself, everyone there sitting at the same table. One night there was a number of lads in to call on us, lads working for other farmers. My fellow farm-servant began to tell a story about the Duke of Argyll. 'He was putting up poles here and there through the hill, beside the main road. Nobody could understand why in the world he was putting these poles up. But at last they found out. It was for the Irishmen, when they came over from Ireland, they would be on the tramp, and when they came to one of these posts, they would be scratching themselves and saying, 'God bless the Duke of Argyll, put up these posts'.[2]

Off he went. The Irishman took out his knife, and would have stuck the knife in him if he hadn't fled. But we couldn't help laughing, when we heard the use the posts were being put to!

The Bicycle without Brakes

When I was working for Tommy MacDonald on Loch Tummel-side, there was a lad from Stonybridge in Uist working for a farmer up at Loch Rannoch at a place called Dalarich, half-way up the loch. He used to write to me and ask me to go and look him up. Well, he was a long way away from me, more than twenty miles before I'd reach him. The other farm-servant along with me had a bicycle. I asked him if he would lend me the bicycle for a day, for Sunday, for me to try to go to see the lad from Uist. He said he would.

It was a fine Sunday, my Sunday off, and I got his bicycle and went off. There was an hotel on the way, and I went into it to see if I could get a drop of whisky. Oh, I couldn't—well, I could get a dram, and I'd have to sign my name in the book. I said that it wasn't a dram that I wanted at all, that I wanted a bottle or a half-bottle, I was going to see a friend.

'Oh, very well,' he said, 'I think you'll get that, then.'

He gave me a half-bottle. I put it in my pocket. After I had left the hotel, I had a fine road up the loch, and then there came a piece of level road. The bicycle that I had had no brakes at all. Then I saw a post standing beside the road, with a board on it, with big red letters on it. I was going at a good speed on the level road, and when I was going past the board, I raised my eyes and what did I see but DANGER FOR BICYCLES with the picture of a hand and forefinger pointing down the brae! I looked ahead and saw the same brae; and I tried to turn back or get off. But the bicycle was gaining speed on me all the time. At last I had to lift my two feet off the pedals and let the bicycle go ahead.

I could see the road go out of sight at the bottom of the brae, and I knew there was a sharp turn there. I was watching the road, and I thought it was coming up towards me with the speed with which I was going down the brae. I was saying to myself that this was my last minute, that I couldn't try to make the turn, the bicycle would skid and my brains would be knocked out against the wall; there was a stone wall on each side of the road. But fortunately what was there but a sand quarry just at the turn. All I did was to let the bicycle run right into the quarry; it took me up to the top of the quarry, and I got off there. When I got off, I was very happy, and I just walked a mile down the road before I got on the bicycle again.

When I reached the farm where my friend was, he had just come home; he had been down at Kinloch Rannoch, and no doubt he was glad to see me, and we were together all day Sunday. Then I got back in the evening, and I was pleased I went, but indeed, when I reached that accursed brae there, I walked all the way coming back. I said to myself that I wouldn't risk it again!

The Lady of Fincastle

This lady used to give a day's sports to everyone on her estate. Her name was Mrs Barber. The farmers were taken there first. There was a hall in front of the castle, and it was in the hall that the farmers were entertained; and the farm-servants were entertained in the castle. I asked Thomas MacDonald why she was taking the farm-servants into the castle, and entertaining the farmers in the hall.

'Ah, I don't know,' he said. 'I think it for fear you'll believe she's looking down on you, that that's it. But instead of that she's looking on you far above us.'

Well, we had to be there at nine in the morning, at the castle, and we didn't get away until six in the evening, and she used to take everyone who hadn't been there before through the castle to see every room in it. But the folk who lived on her estate had seen it before and knew it well enough.

Well, when they were leaving at six o'clock, she used to take them to the front door. She had two daughters. There were two libraries inside beside the front door, with nothing but books on shelves to be seen. She used to give every one of us a book, any book that you chose, and write her name in it, 'A Present from Mistress Barber'; and I'll swear that it was costing her plenty. The book I got, the book I asked for, was a story-book. I didn't keep it long, it was pinched from me in the bothy. But though they pinched the book, they left me plenty of other things. That's the way they were dealing with me.

When we were at the castle, we used to play football in the grounds, some of us, and others used to go for a sail in dinghies on the loch above, if we liked. The girls used to get a drive to Pitlochry. They had to be punctual. Mrs Barber and her daughters were so busy serving them. I think we liked best the fun she was making of them, laughing; there would be plenty of things on the table which they had no idea how they should start to eat! She would be bursting with laughter! Everyone whom she saw looking a bit shy, she would come behind them and pat them on the back, asking them to help themselves, and there was no poor creature on her estate,

73

poor person, old man or woman, but that she used to go to see them on her own feet, giving them presents every year. She was good to them indeed; a fine woman.

The Tramp at Borenich

The autumn I was working for Tommy MacDonald on Loch Tummel-side, workers were very scarce, and this fellow came around at harvest-time, to see if he could get work. My word, they were very glad, he wasn't old either, I'd say he wasn't much more than thirty. The boss told him that he could give him work for the autumn, and he was content. This day was a holiday they used to keep, and we weren't doing anything. But the tramp was finding it a long time to be idle, not working. He was miserably clad, and his shoes were no better.

I had shoes which had become hard. I put soles on them and gave them to him. I gave him socks and a dungaree jacket. The other farm-servant gave him a shirt and trousers and drawers and a cap. We dressed him up and shaved him; and when he went in for dinner the women didn't recognize him at all, they didn't know who it was. We made great fun of them that they didn't recognize the tramp. We made a bed for him in the stable loft, and he was going to stay with us all the autumn, and my word! we were glad of the help we were going to get.

Next morning, I and the other lad were in the stable, when we were just ready to go in for our breakfast, I took a pitchfork and struck the ceiling under the tramp's bed to awaken him. I shouted to him to get up and come down. I didn't hear anyone moving. We went in to our breakfast. When we had gone in and sat down at the table, the master asked:

'Did you wake the fellow?'

'I did,' I said.

The tramp didn't come in.

'Look and see if the fellow's alive, as he hasn't come in. Are you sure you woke him?'

'Well, I think I woke him,' I said. 'I rattled the ceiling with the handle of the pitchfork, but I didn't hear anyone moving.'

We went out and I went up the stair; I was afraid to look, in case he was dead in bed. I looked, and there was no sign of the tramp; but the two worn-out shoes he had been wearing were in the loft. There was no sign of himself. I came down and told the master there was no sign of him. Oh dear, how ashamed he was! The tramp had asked him for an advance of five shillings, as he had no tobacco; he had given it to him. When the tramp had got the five shillings, he had made off with them.

Three years afterwards I was at Rowardennan. It was a rough winter night and snow was falling, sleet. When I was going to bed, shutting the bothy door, I heard a knock at the door, and I looked and there was a man there. He was asking for shelter, and you could hardly have understood him for the cold.

'Oh,' I said, 'you can't have shelter.' I didn't dare to let anyone in the door there, the place wasn't insured. 'You can't get shelter here, clear off.' I shut the door.

'Oh,' he said, 'for God's sake give me some kind of shelter.'

'Oh well, I'll do anything for that. Wait there a minute now, then.'

I went inside and put on my boots and lit a lantern. I came out. 'Come along this way, then. Follow me.'

He went along with me. I opened the stable door. There was a bale of straw in the stable, and there was a stall there with no animal in it. I went in and spread the bale of straw in the empty stall.

'There you are now,' I said. 'Have you tobacco?'

'Yes,' he said.

'Have you matches?'

'I did have, but they're wet.'

'Have you a pipe?'

'I have.'

'Well, you must give the pipe and the tobacco and everything of that sort to me. You're not going to set this place on fire.'

'Oh, the matches I've got won't set anything on fire,' he said. He put his hand in his pocket and took out a handful of matches, dripping wet.

75

'Oh, go along,' I said, 'if they're no better than that, you're safe enough.'

I gave him horse-rugs to cover himself with. He took off every stitch of clothing he had on,[3] and hung them on a stall there. He was all right when he got his wet clothes off. At six o'clock next morning, I got up and went along to the stable. He had woken up. I called to him to get up and clear off as quick as he could. He got up and began to get dressed; he was looking at me now and again while I was cleaning out the stable. Standing in the door, he said:

'I believe I've seen your face before.'

'I don't know. I don't believe I've seen yours.'

'Were you at work on Loch Tummel-side three years ago, with Tommy MacDonald?'

'I was,' I said.

'I was sure I'd seen you. Well, you did me a good turn then, and you did me a good turn last night, or I wouldn't be alive today. But you're getting on very well, but no better than you deserve.'

It was then I thought of the tramp to whom I gave the boots; and I would have said he was twenty years older than when I saw him before, so much had he aged.

'Well, I don't believe you're much better off than when I saw you.'

'Oh, I'm not,' he said.

That's how I found the tramp; but didn't he recognise me well, though!

5

ROWARDENNAN

How I Went to Work for Mr Kane

IN THE springtime I left home. Work was not plentiful at the time, there was only a little to be had. I went to Oban and started working with stonemasons who were building a church. The pay was poor, only fourpence halfpenny an hour, some men were getting fivepence an hour; fivepence half-penny an hour was the highest that was going for a labourer.

I didn't look like putting much by there to send home, so I engaged with a hotelkeeper on Loch Lomond, an Irishman called Edward Kane. It was springtime when I first went to the hotel, to Rowardennan; the farm-servant who had been there before me was from Fort William, and he had left at Martinmas; no one stayed there longer than six months, I was the person who stayed longest there. Kane had a shepherd's son as a guide for people going up to the top of Ben Lomond with ponies in the summer; he had kept him on all through the winter, and had not been thinking of getting a farm-servant before the beginning of spring.

At this time I was working at the pier at Oban, and I was watching the papers to see if I could find a place; I was only waiting for the first place I could find, to leave, as I saw that the day would never come when I could save a penny at Oban. Anyway, I saw this place advertised in the paper, looking for a ploughman, who could take charge of all the out-door work, a man who must be good at ploughing and at scything and at working with boats. Well, I was fit for all these things. I applied for it, and in two days there came a telegram from Kane telling me to come along, the situation was awaiting me.

I went off. When I arrived, Kane's son William met me at the pier, with the shepherd's son I've mentioned, he was on the pier too. William asked me if I was the man for the hotel, and I said I was.

'Come this way, then,' he said. 'Rob will take your case up. Come along.'

I came in. William went along to the bar and said I had arrived, and the old man came up. He talked to me for a while in the kitchen, and asked me why I hadn't come yesterday when he sent the wire for me. I said I had been working in Oban, and that today had been our pay-day, and that was why I had not come yesterday.

'Oh, well,' he said, 'that'll be all right.'

The other fellow, Rob, used to go along to the bar every night at ten o'clock[1] to ask the boss for orders. Well, there were no orders for him to go and ask for once I had arrived, as I was in charge of all the work outside. I listened to him without saying anything, but my word! it annoyed me right enough. I was saying to myself that I would have to speak some day, but that I would let things be for the present.

Kane used to come out to talk to me, and I was complaining how far back the work was, nothing had been done, not a cartload of manure had been put out, not a furrow had been turned, the land for the turnips that should have been ploughed during the winter was untouched.

'Oh, well,' he said, 'I hadn't anyone to plough it; you are getting on very well, you've got a good helper in Rob; though he can't plough, he can do other work.'

'Oh, yes,' I said, 'but that won't do the ploughing that should have been done by now.'

'Oh, well, that can't be helped this year,' said Kane.

Things went on like this, and pity's the turn I was getting from Rob at all; every day after breakfast he used to give me the slip some way or other. One day he was along with me in the stable after breakfast, and I told him to harness a horse to a cart and start putting out the manure that was there. That was all right, and I went off to plough; I didn't see a glimpse of

Rob. When I came home at nightfall, one of the ponies in the stable was missing. I realized that Rob had gone off with it somewhere. I went in for my supper, and asked where Rob Baird was. One of the servant-girls answered that he had gone up to the top of Ben Lomond with a pony and a gentleman.

'When did he go there?' I asked.

'Oh, it was after three o'clock when he left,' she said.

The barmaid was standing at the head of the table, watching me steadily.

'I thought you were the man, Angus, when you came here.'

'Isn't that what I am, a man?' I said.

'Oh, I know that, but I see Rob's the man, and not you.'

'Oh, Rob's a man, all right.'

'Yes, and Rob's giving you orders instead of you giving them to him,' she said.

'Oh, poor Rob isn't giving me orders,' I said. 'I know what I ought to do.'

'Oh, you needn't say that to me. I've heard him giving them to you.'

'Oh,' I said, 'if that pleases him, it doesn't harm me.'

'Well,' she said, 'the sooner you put a stop to that, the better for you,' she said, going off in a rage when she saw how indifferent I was about it, when she was telling me.

'My word,' I said to myself, 'you must be hearing more than I am.' But I didn't let on at all.

A day or two afterwards, a new range came that was to be put in the kitchen; the old one was to be taken out, and hot plates were to be put in; they were going to have the kitchen completely done over. A man came over from Stirling to install it; he was only dodging around the house all the afternoon. When I came home I found out who he was.

That was all there was to it, but that night, at ten o'clock, Rob arose and went along to the bar as usual. I went off to go to bed. Rob came in.

'Are you asleep, Angus?' he said.

'No.'

'You'll have to get up early tomorrow.'

'What's on tomorrow?'

'You've got to take a cart down to Balmaha tomorrow to get

79

sixty fire-bricks, the boss wants you to go there before breakfast so that you'll be back by nine o'clock to let the man who came from Stirling make a start putting in the range. He's being paid from the time he left home until he goes back, whether he's working or not.'

'He's certainly well off,' I said. 'But what are you going to be at tomorrow?'

'Oh, indeed, I won't be idle. I've to take two commercial travellers to the station from the hotel to catch the one o'clock train.'

My word, when I heard this, it made me furious, 'You going off with my horses,' I thought, 'which I'm feeding and cleaning, and I only to be a groom for you; you went off on hires twice before this and I didn't say a word'—I was thinking it was the boss himself who had told him to do this, so as not to stop me ploughing. I didn't say anything, but I turned over in bed, and I didn't get up until it was five o'clock, as usual. I called to Rob to get up, and to the other 'cowboy' who was along with him. I was getting dressed, but they weren't getting up. When I was ready to go out, I called to them again pretty crossly to get out of there, that that wouldn't do.

I went down to the stable and gave some oats to the horses, and went to give them hay. Then Rob came into the stable, bringing the wheelbarrow. I came down, and gave him a fork. I began to lift the horses' bedding.

'Oh, well,' Rob said, 'if you're going to Balmaha now, Angus, you needn't wait to do the stable. I'll clean it out myself.'

'That's what you should do,' I said, 'it should be cleaned out for me on days before I get out of bed to it.'

He didn't say anything. We cleaned out the stable, and I began to clean the horses. When I had finished cleaning them, I looked at the clock, and it was then twenty minutes before breakfast-time; we didn't get our breakfast until half past six. I went and sat down on the grain chest. Rob came and sat down on the chest beside me.

'Are you going to Balmaha now, Angus?' he said.

'I'm damned sure I'm not.'

'Well, you're absolutely right,' he said. 'It's all very well to be asking a man to go off at this hour, but they should give you a cup of tea first.'

I didn't say a word, I let him be.

Breakfast-time came then, and we went in to our breakfast. After breakfast I went out to the stable. Rob came after me. I went in and began to harness the horses for ploughing, to go to plough. Rob stood in the stable door.

'Aren't you going to Balmaha at all?' he asked.

'I never heard a word about Balmaha,' I said. 'You can go there if you want to.'

'Why, you —— ——' he said, 'you can't deny I told you about it yesterday.'

'Are you my master, you bitch's bastard? Clear out of my sight or I'll whitewash the wall with your brains! I'm fed up with your orders. That's enough of them!'

Rob rushed off out of the door, and went up to the house. I went off with the horses. There was a field beside the hotel, and I began to plough there. The boss didn't get up until nine o'clock. When it was past nine, what did I see but Mr Kane coming out, and Rob with him. They came straight over to where I was in the field, Rob holding forth on the way. I didn't let on that I saw them. When Kane was near me, he shouted to me, as I didn't stop.

'Didn't Rob tell you yesterday that a cart would have to go to Balmaha today before breakfast so as to be back by nine o'clock, to get bricks? Yon man who's come over is getting big wages from me for going around with his hands in his pockets doing nothing. What do you mean by it? Are you trying to rob me?'

'Well, I didn't hear that, Mr Kane,' I said, 'but I heard Rob say to me that I had to go to Balmaha before breakfast, and that he himself would be loafing around here sitting in the pantry until he went to catch the one o'clock train. But if Rob's my master, I've been here long enough, there they are for you,' I said, throwing down the reins, 'go where you like with them!'

'Oh, hell,' Kane said, when he saw me throwing down the reins. 'No, Rob has nothing to do with you: I'm your master.'

'Well, that was what I understood when I came here, but I see that Rob's my master and not you; he's giving me orders instead of you. Are you asking me to put a pair of horses indoors and to go to Balmaha with a cart and leave this fellow idle? You said he was a good help for me. All the help I'm getting from him is that he's going like a parrot[2] between you and me. Go and get a farm-servant!' I said, going off to get my jacket.

Kane shouted to me 'Hoy!' and 'hey! Listen to me!' he said.

'I'll listen. What have you to say?'

'Well,' he said, 'I'll tell you. I told Rob last night to tell you that a cart had to go to Balmaha to get bricks, and that a vehicle had to go to the station to catch the one o'clock train, and that you would know who could best go there. I'm not taking anything to do with your work at all, I put you in charge the day you came here, I told you you had to look after all the outside work, I was only——'

'Well, there's a big difference between that and the orders I got,' I said. 'What's keeping Rob from going to Balmaha? I haven't kept him from going. He could have been back by now.'

Kane turned and raised his stick over Rob's head. 'You devil,' he said, 'I told you last night——' he said, lifting his stick. Oh, all Rob did was to turn round and make off for the stable. Kane went off after him. What a cursing he gave him then! He didn't ask him to go at all, but 'Get to hell out of my sight!' Rob went off and harnessed the other horse, and went down the road, and I saw him standing up in the cart with the horse trotting!

A little later I saw Kane coming again.

'Well,' he said, 'that fellow's gone.'

'About time,' I said.

'Yes, it was. The dirty rascal, it's no wonder he put me in a state of nerves today. He came in to see me and said you wouldn't allow a horse or a cart to go there. What a rogue! He wanted to save himself the trouble!'

'Well, I had no one who could take a cart there unless I went myself.'

'He was keeping an easy job for himself,' said Kane.

'He's always doing that,' I said.

'You keep him at work, and if he doesn't do what you tell him to, let me know, it wouldn't take much to make me send him packing.'

'I'll keep him at work if you'll keep him out of the pantry,' I said. 'You know very well I can't go to look for him and leave a pair of horses standing idle here.'

'By God,' Kane said, 'he won't get to sit in the pantry after this. I'll let him see that. I came over to you; you'll have to untie before dinner-time, before midday, the station is ten miles away by the road around, but if you can get through the Duke's policies, it would save you a mile, but that's only a chance. If the gate's closed you'll have to go round. It's a private road, but they won't say anything to us if we go through.'

'All right,' I said, 'if I untie at half past eleven, leaving here, I'll be early enough.'

'Well, you'll have to do that, there's nothing better than being early. That's the best thing of all.'

'All right,' I said, 'what vehicle shall I take? shall I take the single harness or the double harness?'

'Take the double harness, Angus, I'll make them pay for it!'

He went off, and I came in with the horses. I harnessed the two other horses, and put them in the carriage, and came to the front door. I got a cup of tea before I left, and then I made for the station. When I came back in the evening I didn't see a sign of Rob. I was ploughing for a while after I came back. When I came back with the horses, he was in the stable, sweeping it out. My word, I said to myself, this is something new! I'd never seen him in the stable before myself since I'd gone there. He didn't say a word, and neither did I. Then we went in for our supper, and when we had had our supper, I got up and went out to the bothy. Rob got up and followed me.

'What sort of folk did you have today, Angus?' he said.

'Oh, they weren't bad sorts,' I said.

'I'm sure you got a couple of shillings from them,' he said.

83

'If you doubled it, you would be nearer.'

'You don't often come across that kind.'

'If they turned up now and then,' I said, 'it wouldn't be so bad.'

'Well, it was me that should have got that,' Rob said.

'Aye,' I said, 'what way should you have got that?'

'When I stayed here for the winter, I was promised every hire I could take, and it's that I was depending on, I was only getting small wages.'

'Oh, indeed,' I said. 'Did you see his advertisement in the newspaper before I came here, when he was looking for a ploughman?'

'Yes.'

'Did you see that I was to have that, when I came to the place, and was to be in charge of all the outside work? Did you say anything to him then?'

'No,' Rob said. 'I thought it was only something that the man in the newspaper office had put in.'

'Very well then, you go in where he is and make a stand for your bargain. And if he breaks the bargain he made with me, I'll leave tomorrow, and you'll have everything. Go along now, go in to him.'

'Oh well, I won't,' Rob said, 'but he won't do it to me again.'

'Well, you're slack, if you had that bargain with him. Who had the hires last year? You or Archie who was here?'

'I never got to go with a hire as long as Archie was here.'

'Didn't you know that I was to do exactly what Archie was doing? You've gone off with two hires already since I came here, without telling me you were going. But after this, you'll not harness a horse I've brushed; remember that. Do you think I came here to be a groom for you to be cleaning and feeding horses for you to be driving? Are you trying to sit on me, if so take heed you've got the wrong man!'

He choked with anger, but he didn't say a word! Ever after that day he was ready to do everything, even if I had told him to jump in the sea!

Rob Baird and William's Wife

Mr Kane, the Irishman for whom I worked at Rowardennan' had taken a little farm called Ross for his son William, three miles south of the hotel. William was married; he and his wife lived in the farmhouse at Ross. They had no family. William and his father were completely at odds with each other; William had married against his father's wish, he had run away with one of his father's servant-girls, and before his father caught up with them, they had been married by special licence in Glasgow.

I had only been at Rowardennan for a fortnight, when I had to go down to Ross to plough. I took took Rob Baird with me to scatter the molehills before I began to plough; the field was very bad with molehills.

When we had gone part of the way, Rob said to me:

'I don't care much to be coming along here.'

'Why?' I said. 'You needn't think I'm going to be terribly hard on you, after all.'

'Oh, that's not it at all,' he said.

'I think it's better for you to be here than working within sight of the window there,' I said.

'Oh, indeed, I'd sooner be anywhere than coming down here.'

Well, I didn't say any more to him, but when we got there— we took our food with us, and it was William's wife who had to give us our dinner. She was living there. I went in with the basket. She asked me was there anyone along with me. I said there was, that Rob Baird was along with me. She didn't say a word. I went out to plough. After a little while she came out and asked me when I wanted my dinner. I said that any time that suited her would suit me.

'Very well,' she said, 'you'll ask Rob to go home for his dinner.'

'Didn't his dinner come along here at all?'

'If it did,' she said, 'I'm not going to prepare it for him. He'll go home for his dinner.'

I said to myself that I was not going to ask Rob to go home for his dinner, she could ask him. When she had dinner ready,

85

she came out and called to me. Rob and I went over to the house when we had put the horses in. There was a table in the kitchen, and there was a plateful of soup at the end of the table, and a chair there; there was another chair at the other end of the table, and there was nothing there. I went past and sat down at the other end, and Rob sat down on the chair that had the plate in front of it.

In a moment she turned across and lifted the plate from in front of him and put it at my end. 'Get out,' she said, 'and get your dinner where you're telling your lies since the year began.'

'Well, it would be difficult to tell a lie about you,' he said, turning to her, 'I think you could be called anything. If I'm wanting my dinner it's not from you I'm wanting it.'

'Well, if it isn't,' she said, 'go and get it from the people you're working for.'

The row started: and I'd sooner than anything I ever saw have been outside! The grace I had (before my dinner) was a poor one. Anyway, I made haste to get away. Then she asked me if I was going to take tea afterwards, and I said I wasn't, indeed.

'Well, you needn't think anything of this,' she said. 'When you're as knowing of Rob as you're ignorant now, you'll know what kind he is.'

'What have you got to say about me, you devil's bitch?' said Rob.

I got up and went out, and Rob came out after me. There wasn't anything bad that he wasn't saying to her. When I got out, 'My God, Rob,' I said, 'why were you saying that, she might take you to court?'

'Ho! I'll prove everything I said to her,' he said.

'Oh, if you'll prove it, I don't ask for more,' I said. 'I hope it won't go farther than this. What are you going to do now? Are you going to work here fasting?'

'Oh well,' he said, 'I don't mind for one day.'

'Well, you're very foolish,' I said. 'Go and get your dinner where you're working. I don't mind if you don't come here till four in the afternoon. Off you go now.'

'All right, I think that's best for me.'

Rob went off and made for the hotel. In the afternoon he returned. I asked him, 'Did you see the boss, when you were up there?'

'Oh, I didn't,' he said.

'Did he know you'd gone back for your dinner?'

'I'm sure he did.'

'Oh, well, indeed,' I said, 'I'll see about it when I get home.'

When I had come home, I was in the kitchen. The boss sent the barmaid to fetch me. I went along.

'How did you get on today?' he said.

'I got on very well.'

'Are you going down there tomorrow?'

'I am.'

'Will you be taking Rob with you tomorrow?'

'I'll need him down there tomorrow as much as I needed him today,' I said.

'It's bad with molehills,' he said.

'It is, indeed,' I said. 'But Rob can't do much work if he has to be coming back for dinner every day.'

'Mistress Kane wouldn't give him his dinner at all?'

'Indeed she wouldn't,' I said.

'Oh, she must give him his dinner,' he said. 'She's getting paid for it. I'll speak to William, she must give him his dinner.'

'Indeed,' I said, 'I'd think so.'

Next day, we went down again, and I took Rob with me. I sent the basket into her as usual. She asked me, 'Is Rob here today along with you?'

'He is,' I said.

'Perhaps he's the better for what he got yesterday?'

'Well, I believe it would do for one day, anyway.'

When it was dinner-time, she came out and called to me that dinner was ready. We put the horses in, and went over to the house. When we were just at the door, she came out with Rob's dinner, and put it down on the doorstep, and, 'Eat it there, or else take it away with you! You won't get in!'

All he could do was to take it with him over to the stable; and he never got dinner or supper or anything else inside the door as long as I was there! Every day he was down there along with me, he was given his dinner at the door just like a dog, she wouldn't let him inside the house. I always used to say to him that he had little self respect when he was taking it from her like that.

'Just you wait,' he said, 'you'll get your dinner outside yet, just as sure as me. The lad who was here before you, Archie, he was as I am today, getting his dinner outside, and I was getting mine indoors; you'll be doing the same yet.'

'By the Book, she won't ever give me dinner outside; if she does, she'll only do it once!'

That's how I left Rob and William's wife, indeed they weren't of the best sort of folks!

Loch Lomond

When I was working on Loch Lomond-side, we had five miles of the loch in which we could trawl for fish for the hotel, from the laird. And there were plenty of other fish besides salmon; there was a fish like what we call '*bodach ruadh*'—codling;[3] and there was another fish like the wrasse, which I used to see on the east coast of Uist here; but these were white.[4] Well, they weren't making any use of these, they used to throw them back. And there were herrings there, fresh-water herrings;[5] 'powans' was the name they had for them in English. These used to be as thick as I ever saw them in the Minch; sometimes we used to get them in the trawl, and would have to let them out and not take them ashore at all, but empty it. They weren't making much use of these, sometimes they would take five or six of them home, and the cook would likely fry them, but indeed they didn't taste like herring; they tasted of fresh water to me. That's the kind of fishing there was.

There were plenty of salmon, and some days we would get what we needed pretty near at hand, and others we would be trawling half the day and getting nothing. But there was one place to the south which the laird[6] was keeping for himself, where nobody was to go, but we used to slip in secretly sometimes, and we would get fish there any time we went there. One turn drawing the trawl would do, and we would have plenty. The laird didn't know we were going near it.

The loch was fearfully deep; I believe there's one piece they've never found the bottom of at all. And they used to tell me that a boat had been wrecked there, and there was a lady on board, and she had a trunk with a lot of jewellery in it, and the trunk had been found again on the sea shore, so that there must be a tunnel going out of the loch to the sea. That's the way they made it out, there was a piece of the loch where they never found the bottom at all, so that there must be a tunnel going out, going to the sea.

Many people were drowned in the same loch. Three people were drowned while I was there myself; a shepherd to the north of us, called Angus MacFadyen, was drowned; and another fellow who came from Edinburgh, when they came out on a tour, two hundred and fifty of them. There were two brothers, who came to try to hire a boat; they got one. They were charging a shilling an hour for a hire. The brothers went over to the other side of the loch with her; within an hour we got word that the elder of them had been drowned. The game-keeper and I went off then, and we found him; he wasn't far from land at all, but if he had been two yards farther out, we would never have got him, with the depth there was. All there was for it was to make the poor fellow's coffin and put him in it and tie his clothes on top of it, and send him back to his folk; the poor man.

Another man was drowned crossing the loch, the first year I went there—on the ice. A lot of money had been promised to the first person who crossed the loch on the ice, on skates; he went off—he was one of the Colquhouns—and he went through the ice and was drowned. When the thaw came, they got a diver to try to find his body. Well, the diver went down, and came up; they asked him if he had seen him. 'I did,' he said. 'I saw him, and the devil eel has got a hold of him, and though I got all the money of the Colquhouns, I wouldn't go down again!'

One of the steamers once went aground on a sandbank, all summer long, down by Balmaha, between Balmaha and Rowardennan. Every Sunday there would be at least twenty dinghies around her, there was drink aboard and everything, in the bar, nothing had been put out of her, and the steward was aboard her all the time. She was there until the autumn rains came and the loch rose, and then she got off. They were trying to take her off with another steamer, and couldn't manage to do it, she was only sinking in the sand all the time. There were sandbanks there just as you can see off the west of Uist and what is very strange is that there are waves on the loch every day of the year, though there wasn't a breath of wind; there is a swell[8] on the loch like you see on the shore here; there is.

Once there was an Englishman in the hotel, and the Boots, a cheeky lad[9] from Aberfoyle, was out with him in a dinghy, and the steamer was going past. When the swell from the steamer came on the dinghy, it was rocking from side to side. 'Oh,' said the Englishman, 'it's a long time since I heard that there were three wonderful things in Loch Lomond; waves without wind, fish without fins, and a floatin' island.'[10]

'Oh, that's true,' said the Boots.

The Englishman turned to the Boots. 'Where's the floatin' island?'[10] he said.

'Well, it was here yesterday,' said the Boots, 'but I don't know where it is today!'

'Oh, that'll do you, Scottie!'[10] said the Englishman.

The Poachers

At this time there was a man from Dumbarton called Sandy Blair working along with me cutting hay. We were inside at our tea when the boss came in and said that there wasn't a bit of fish in the house and that we would have to go out with the net. Well, this was all right, but I was very loathe to go when I had hay ready to put up in cocks; but I had to go. The boss used to give us a bottle of whisky and sandwiches every night we went, while we were away.

When we had gone down to the boat and were putting the net aboard, we found a fearful hole in it. The hotel would have gone through the hole in the net.

'Oh, well,' I said, 'let the fishing be tonight. I haven't got time to mend that tonight.'

'That's the work of poachers,' said Sandy Blair.

'No one ever took it poaching,' I said.

'Yes, plenty did,' he said.

'The boat couldn't be moved on the rollers without my noticing.'

'It's funny you didn't notice it, then. Many a night they went out with her last year, and me along with them.'

'Who was going out with her?' I asked.

'Folk who've been in your company often enough.'

'No,' I said, 'it's you who are tearing it when you're dragging it, you don't care whether there's a stone in it or not in your hurry to pull it ashore.'

'Oh, no,' said Blair. 'It's the poachers, that's who it is.'

I didn't say any more. We could only go back. Kane asked us what was wrong that we hadn't gone. His son William told him that the net had been torn, and that Blair was saying that poachers had been going out with it, and that they had been going out with it last year.

I would have liked to have boiled Blair! Never mind, it couldn't be helped. That night we were called to the bar. Kane said we must set a watch, and that two of us in turn must wait to see if we could catch the persons who were taking out the boat.

'Oh, well,' I said, 'no one will take her out tonight, anyway, the net's no use until it's been mended.'

'Well,' said Kane, 'see and mend it first thing in the morning, and when you've got it finished, try a turn down there at the island, off the pier, and see if you can get enough fish for dinner.'

'All right,' I said.

In the morning I began to mend the net, and it took me until eleven o'clock. We tried a turn with it at the end of the island, and we got twelve sea trout and two salmon. That was a good catch for one turn. We took them ashore and brought them to the hotel. Kane was pleased then without a doubt. He emptied them into a trough of water behind the kitchen and took everyone in the hotel out to see how pretty they looked in the water.

When we had had our supper that evening, he came along.

'Well,' he said, 'now two of you must wait tonight, and another two of you tomorrow night.'

No one knew who was going to do it.

'Well,' he said, turning to his son William, 'you and Sandy Blair will go together, then, and Angus and Johnny MacLaren' (a lad who was looking after the cattle), 'they'll go together, and Rob and the Boots; that's three watches. They'll take a night in turn to see who they'll catch.'

Lots were cast then to see who would wait tonight. The lot fell on William and Blair to wait up the first night; the next night it was to be Johnny and me, and the third night the other two fellows.

'Keep at it like that,' said Kane, 'until you catch them.'

William and Blair sat up all night and were back and forth between the hotel and the net, and didn't see anybody. I had to watch the next night. It was a beautiful clear night, and I said to myself that if a poacher were to come, it would be tonight that he would do it. Johnny MacLaren was along with me sitting beside the range, beginning to get sleepy.

'I think you're falling alseep, Johnny.'

'Well, I am,' he said.

'Off with you to bed!'

'Who'll be along with you?'

'If I need you, I'll wake you up. Off with you. You can do the stable for me in the morning and let me get an hour's sleep.'

'I will, indeed, but you wake me,' he said.

'I'll wake you sure enough. Off with you!'

Johnny went off, and I was alone then. I said to myself that I didn't care if they scraped it from one end to the other. There was no one but myself there. I was beginning to fall asleep myself. It was getting on for dawn. I got up and went outside. The night was as quiet as could be. I heard the sound of rowing down in the bay where the boat was. I went down quietly. The boat was just in at the foot of the bank, after coming back, with four men in her. I stopped and stood behind a tree on the bank of the loch. The boat came in on the sand just in front of me. One of the men got out of her, with his trousers rolled up. He started to pull her. The others made

92

1. Angus in the Militia (from a photograph taken in 1889).

2. Angus opening the drills.

3. Tirine.

4. The Lime Kiln.

5. Borenich.

6. Rowardennan Hotel.

7. Rowardennan. Angus (centre), the Barmaid, Kitchen-maid, and Johnny MacLaren (on left).

8. Loch Lomond looking northward from Rowardennan.

9. The field at Ross where Angus nearly shot the cow by mistake for a deer.

10. The old coach stable at Dalmally Hotel. The Hotel itself has been burnt down and rebuilt since Angus worked there.

her list over to one side.[11] When they were within reach, I jumped down to the water from behind the tree. The three men who were in the boat jumped out of her and went off through the water leaving a white wake, over to a plantation on the other side of the bay.

The man who was pulling up the boat went wild; he looked to each side and didn't see anything, then he looked behind him, and I was standing there! Off he went after the others; I was there before him; he was slower in the water than I was on land. Every attempt he made I was there before him. Whenever he stopped, he turned his back to me; and for pity's sake who had I got but Johnny MacIntyre the forester's son who lived a bit down the loch; he had been calling on me earlier in the evening!

'Oh, come ashore, Johnny,' I said, 'you needn't stay out there, or else I'll keep you out till the sun rises.'

'It looks as if you would,' he said. He came ashore.

'Go and bring in the rope, I'm not going to get myself wet.'

He went and brought the rope.

'Who's along with you?' Oh, that was something I couldn't find out. My word, but he was close!

'You can just as well tell me!'

'I won't.'

'I'll promise not to tell.'

'We'll leave it at that, then.'

'Oh, go and whistle them,' I said, 'they're only in the plantation over there, see if we can't get the boat pulled up.'

He wouldn't do this, for fear I meant to give them away.

'Damn it,' I said, 'hurry up, it's nearly daytime. No one's up but me. You're all right tonight, but if you had come last night, you wouldn't have been so safe.'

He started to whistle then. Someone came out of the wood, took a couple of steps, and then stopped. For pity's sake who was it but Alec MacGregor,[12] the son of the gamekeeper who lived a bit up the loch from me, and two of the wood-cutters, two Irishmen.

'Upon my word,' I said, 'the sons of foresters and game-keepers poaching! You two are only doing what I'd do myself, but they'll be hung for it![13]

They didn't say a word.

'Here,' I said, 'get a move on and pull her up!'

We pulled the boat up then.

'Did you tear the net tonight?'

Oh, they didn't, they'd never gone out with it before to-night, and they wished they'd never done that!

'Aren't you going out with it every night? What's the good of telling me that?'

Oh, no, no, they had never gone out with it!

'Oh no!' I said, 'when it's the one who was along with you last year who gave you away!'

'Who?' they said.

'Why, Blair,' I said.

'Oh, the devil take me,' said one of the Irishmen, 'if I don't go and pull him out of bed by the feet though I were to be hung for it!'

'For God's sake,' I said, 'don't any of you let Blair find out what's happened, in case it's learnt that I told you. I don't care what you do to him when he and I've parted.'

'Well,' said the Irishman, 'I'll take it out on him, even if he's been put in his coffin, I'll take it out on him.'

'Oh, do what you like to him, but don't say a word to him as long as he's here. And take care you don't come poaching again, there's a watch out every night. Since they haven't caught anyone, it won't last terribly long.'

'Well,' the Irishman said, 'we'll do that, we won't say anything for your sake, but we're not saying he's going to get away with it.'

They had a sack, which was nearly full of fish. They were going to go off and leave it. 'Oh, devil's brood,' I said, 'take the sack out of my sight, and I'll try to hide your tracks.'

They took the sack away with them then. I began to hide their footprints with a branch, and I made plenty of footprints myself. Next morning when Kane got up, I hadn't seen any-thing more than the people who'd been there the previous night had.

This went on for a week, and they weren't catching anyone. One evening when I was scything, Kane came out and came over to where we were.

SANDY BLAIR AND THE LOAN

'Well,' he said, 'you're getting on very well with the hay, Angus.'

'That isn't easy,' I said, 'to get on with it. A man who's up all night, can't work in the daytime. The best thing you can do is to leave the job to Blair; he'll earn good wages, he's getting three shillings every night he stays up, and his day's pay over and above, and to sleep till nine o'clock; he'll make a good week's wages. If you believe the lies Blair tells you, he'll tell you enough to thatch a house!'

'Oh, the roof would only be a thin one, Angus!'

'I'm not telling lies,' Blair said.

'What is it but lies? If poachers were going out with the net, it's funny you didn't catch them!'

'They weren't there the night I was there,' he said.

'And were they there the night I was there? If they had been, I'd have caught them. I wouldn't put it past you to have done it yourself, to get yourself a good job.'

'Well, I don't say you aren't right, Angus,' said Kane.

'I am right,' I said. 'I'm not going to be at it any longer, whoever is.'

'Oh well, then,' said Kane, 'that'll do. There will be no more watch on.'

But Blair would have gladly put a bullet in me! But the watch stopped; there was never any more talk of it.

Sandy Blair and the Loan

The boss came one day to ask me when I expected to start cutting the hay. I said I was sure it wouldn't be long.

'Well, it's just about this time they used to start it. Is there a chance of your having anyone to go to the hay along with you?'

'No, indeed,' I said, 'I haven't spoken to anyone.'

'Blair was talking to me, would he get to go along with you to the hay,' he said.

'Oh, all right,' I said.

'Well, then,' said Kane, 'you only have to speak to him any day you're going to start on it.'

'Well, I'm thinking I'll start on it on Monday.'

'Very good,' he said.

This fellow Blair came down with the others to the hotel on Saturday evening. He came to where I was.

'Am I going to get to be along with you at the hay this year?'

'I don't know,' I said. 'I'm sure you are, if you're good at cutting hay.'

Oh yes, he was.

'Well then,' I said, 'you'll only have to come along on Monday.'

He came on Monday. Then he spoke to me could I give him a little money—he had to find lodgings, he couldn't get a place in the hotel at all.

'I must get lodgings,' he said. 'Will you lend me a little money to get shirts and a semmet? I'll need something respectable going to get lodgings.'

Well, upon my word—'What do you need?' I said.

'Oh, I'll need thirty shillings,' he said.

Well, since the man was going to work along with me, this was all right. I gave it to him. Oh, he was pleased enough, but my goodness, I was to repent of it, that he had got a place there.

He now was staying—he got lodgings in William's house; his work was just beside him there. That's where most of the hay was altogether. I had to walk down there, it was three miles around by the road, but there was a short cut through the wood, of a mile and a half, half the distance. The earliest I could get down, it would be after eight o'clock before I arrived; and perhaps I would have to go across the loch with the ferry before I got away in the morning. If I had to do the ferry, it would be nine o'clock before I arrived. That Blair wouldn't do a turn except sit down outside until I came.

The boss used to ask me if Blair was starting at seven in the morning, and I used to say he was; I wasn't going to run him down at all; but I was killing myself doing what he should have been doing. And it wasn't that that was hurting me at last, but that if I was working ten minutes after time, he would be grumbling that he wasn't getting to stop on time. I had to turn on him at last and say, 'You start on time, as you ought to, at seven o'clock in the morning and I'll be able to stop on time, but I'm doing myself the work that you should be doing.'

He didn't say any more, he kept quiet.

Well then, when we were putting in the hay, and the grass had been cut, and everything, Blair had taken a spite towards me, on account of the watch,[14] though he didn't let on. He had been left down at Ross, forking hay into the carts, and I was in the stack-yard at the steading. Each man who came with a cartload, was getting a glass of whisky and a jug of beer. There wasn't any way I could send Blair anything, but at dinner-time I sent him a half-bottle of whisky by Rob, and 'give him that,' I said, 'and tell him I'll remember him when he comes, that he won't miss anything.'

Evening was coming on, and we looked like being finished in good time; there were seven carts carrying hay to the stack. It was a good distance indeed, but upon my soul, the stack was a good size. My helper Rob came along with a cart, and asked me:

'Will I have to go down again, Angus?'

'It's likely you will. And if you bring back as good a cart-load as you have now, that will finish it. The rest can un-harness as they come in.'

He went off with his horse at a trot. But what the hell, he came back—and there were two other carts still to come after him—with the box of his cart full of the bottoms of haycocks, just the bottoms, something that wasn't fit to go into a stack. I cursed him to hell, what for had he brought that along, nobody had told him to.

'Well, I brought along what I was given,' he said.

'It was not what you were given,' I said, 'but what I told you to get that you should have brought; but now you and Blair can go and get a cartload that'll put a finish on the stack; are we going to leave it open like this? What if the rain comes?'

They went off, both pretty cross. But then he and Blair came back, with a good load on the horse, with a cart of fresh grass that I had put up the day before. I was at work dressing the stack with a rake. The first forkload he put up, he said, 'That'll keep your stack warm, Angus.' I came down and tried the hay with my hand. What the devil was it but the fresh grass I had put up yesterday! All I did was to step in front of him.

'What made you bring that along, you damned fool,' I said, 'going to get it from another field? There are still three cocks of the old hay down there!'

'I've brought up what I was given.'

'What you were given! You knew very well that it wasn't that that I needed to go into the stack. Didn't I show you this morning,' I said, turning to Blair, 'the hay that was to be brought up?'

'No, you didn't,' he said.

'I did,' I said.

'You're a liar!'

'I am not, but you are,' I said, 'and it's not your worst fault. But if you don't hold your tongue, I'll come down and knock your brains out on the cartwheel.'

'You come down,' he said.

I lost my temper[15] and jumped from the top of the stack into the cart, and he ran away. I caught him and knocked him flat on his back in the bottom of the haycocks which have been brought up before. I was just going to let him have it[16] before I would let him go. William, the hotelkeeper's son, rushed over and caught hold of me. 'Ah, Angus, Angus!' he said, 'for God's sake let him alone. I know what he is.'

'I'll let him go,' I said, 'indeed I'm not going to dirty my hands with him. But if I had enough time to finish it, you'd go back yet to get another cartload.'

Rob was standing beside the stack with the cart, with the pitchfork under his arm. 'Clear out of there,' I said, turning to him.

'Where'll I go with it?'

'I don't care if you go to hell with it. Go and put it into the shed.'

He went off. All I could do then was to start collecting tarpaulins. I was as humiliated as could be that I had not managed to get the stack finished. Then they went in to supper; no doubt they got plenty of drink. Then Blair went home. Next morning, well—there was another fortnight's work for him there anyway. I went in where they were.

'Well, Angus,' Kane said, 'what are you thinking of doing today?'

'The stack must be finished, anyway,' I said, 'right away.'

'You didn't manage to finish it last night at all.'

'I did not,' I said. 'That was on account of your good farm-servants.'

'Oh, I heard that,' he said. 'You didn't give them enough to drink.'

'Well, I sent a half-bottle down to him along with his dinner.'

'Tut,' he said, 'what use was that? He likes to be blind drunk.'

'Very well,' I said, 'let him get something that blinds him. But are you going to keep him?'

'I'm not going to keep him an hour unless you need him; I don't need him at all myself.'

'Well, if you don't need him at all, I'll manage without him, and I'd much sooner be without him.'

'Has he come?' Kane said.

'He's down towards the house.'

'Go and tell him to come in, then.'

I went out. Blair and Rob were talking at the end of the bothy, with Blair looking so sly.

'What's on today, Angus?' he said.

'Go in and see the boss now,' I said, 'and you'll find out what's on.'

He went off and entered the house. He was inside for a short time. In a minute he came out. He took hold of his jacket and put it on and made off. 'Good day to you, lads,' he said.

Rob looked at him. 'Has Blair left?' he said.

'Yes, it's long since he should have gone,' I said, 'and it would take little for me to send you after him. You were just as much to blame as he was.'

'What had I to do with it?' he said.

'Hadn't you? Weren't you ignorant thinking I didn't know what hay was fit to go into a stack? Off with you now and harness one of the horses down there and go and get a cart to come here, I'm not going to trust you to go by yourself, I'll go down and I'll see what goes into it.'

Rob went off without saying a word. I took the short cut

and was down at Ross before him. 'So,' I said, 'which was the nearer for you, the haycocks that are here now, or going over to the other field to get a cock that would set the stack on fire? You didn't get the chance.'

'Oh,' he said. 'All I did was to take what I found.'

'Oh, no,' I said, 'you two had a plan made, but it didn't work well for you.'

I didn't get a penny of the thirty shillings. Well, I thought now—my fine fellow went off to Glasgow and was away there for a fortnight. Then he came back and started working in the forest, where he was before, for Kennedy. I was there.[17] Then there came the next season. Well, I was afraid now that if I were to keep him out, I would never get a penny of the thirty shillings. The boss asked me if I was willing to take Blair on this year.

'Oh, well,' I said, 'I think that since he did the job last year, he'll do it this one.'

'Oh, well then, you only have to speak to him yourself,' he said.

Blair came that year. We were on good enough terms all the season, but when you got your wages, you hell-hound, you went off, and Angus didn't get a penny. But you'll think I was slack, that all I had to do was to speak a word to the master and he'd keep it off Blair's wages. Well, I didn't like to take his wages, I was thinking that he was honest enough to pay it himself. But you went off, you devil, and made for Glasgow as you did last year. When he came back from there he didn't have a penny, and he started working in the woods, where he had been before.

Well, here I was, leaving at Martinmas. When Blair heard I was leaving, he wasn't coming down near the hotel then. On pay-day he and another fellow took a dinghy across the loch. I didn't know what to do, but it served me right for having let him have it. The time was just a week before the term. Who was in the tap-room but this Kennedy, the man who had the wood, and the forester, a couple of boozers the pair of them. They used to be there all day, and they used to go home in the evening as steady as judges after having been drinking all day.

I was in the kitchen, and Kane called me to come and

answer that bell. I went along. The pair of them were there before me. The forester called for two glasses of whisky and two pints of beer. I came back and asked Kane for them and went and paid for them myself, and took them down to them. The forester started off to pay for them.

'Oh, I've paid for it already,' I said.

'I wanted to stand you a drink,' he said.

'It's like that I'm afraid I won't see you again,' I said, 'I'm leaving.'

'Well, indeed,' said Kennedy, 'I'm very sorry you're leaving. I said to Mr Kane today that I was surprised he was letting you go, and he told me he couldn't do anything to keep you. And I told him I had heard he was reducing your wages. He said he was not, that he was raising your wages, and that you wouldn't accept it.'

'Oh, that's right enough,' I said.

'But I didn't hear it from you,' he said.

'Oh, he was taking something off my wages right enough,' I said, 'but when he offered to restore it it was no use.'

I turned to Kennedy then. 'Will you come out with me for a moment?' I said. 'I've some business with you.'

'Yes,' he said. He got up and came out. 'What is it?'

'One of the men working in your squad up there has owed me something for two years and I know he's not willing to pay it,' I said.

'Who is it?' he said. 'Is it Blair?'

'Yes, just so.'

'Well, I was thinking,' said Kennedy, 'that there was something on that he wasn't coming down here; but I pay them every fortnight and it's next Saturday I'll be paying them. You send me a letter before then, and mention the sum of money you gave him, and the date on which you gave it, and we'll see what the fellow will say.'

My word, I couldn't remember the date on which I'd given him it. I went in to where Kane was and told him.

'Oh, indeed,' he said, 'another idiot. It's one man in a thousand to whom you should lend money, let alone anything else. Why didn't you say a word to me and you would have got it here? I'd have kept it off him.'

'Well, I would have felt it a bad thing to do that.'

'Ho, yes,' he said, 'but he didn't feel it a bad thing to do to you.'

'I've no idea of the date,' I said; 'he began on here the first year.'

'If you haven't, I know very well,' he said. 'Where's that book, Lizzie?' (The barmaid, she was standing by.) She brought over the book. This told the day of the month on which Blair started work last year.

'Get the pen, Lizzie!'

She didn't say another word, Kane knew best what he would put in it.

'Well, send him that,' he said.

Saturday was pay-day. Blair went in. Kennedy took hold of the letter. He read it in the presence of everyone there.

'Is that right,' said Kennedy, turning to Blair.

'Oh, yes, I was going down tonight, I'll give it to him.'

'You've had plenty of nights to give it to him on since you got it,' Kennedy said. 'You won't get the chance now to give it to him tonight. And that's what you're getting, and you won't be doing any more for me, and now clear off.'

When I was at my supper there was a knocking at the door. The kitchenmaid went down and who was there but Kennedy. He asked if I was in. She said I was.

'Tell him I've business with him.'

She came back. 'Kennedy is at the door, Angus, and wants to see you.'

I got up and went along. Kennedy was at the door. He put his hand in his pocket and held out the thirty shillings to me. 'Here,' he said. 'I've given him the sack, I've sent him off.'

'By God,' I said, 'I didn't ask for that.'

'Well, no, but if I did it, it was only what he deserved. It'll show him he should take the clean road in future.'

I got the thirty shillings, but if it hadn't been for Kennedy, I never would have got them!

How I Unloaded the Puffer

One day when Blair and I were cutting hay, the reaper broke down. All we had was the scythes. Whenever there was a fine day and I wanted to leave the hay dry for putting up and needed help, oh, the boss couldn't give me helpers, there was a lot of people in the hotel, and he would have wanted me myself if I could have stayed. 'But you get the hay cut, and you'll get plenty of people to put it up.'

I and Blair were cutting, and we used to stop in the evening, and put up a few cocks; there was a lot of hay on the ground. Then I had it nearly all cut but for one day's work. This day, a Saturday, I got up in the morning, oh, there had been very good drying weather all night, with an east wind, everything was so dry, and we had a good bit ready to put up in big stacks. When I had had my breakfast, I went along to the bar, and asked the barmaid if the boss had got up, and she said he hadn't, that he'd been a while there. I went up to see him. He asked what was wrong. I said nothing, that it was a good day for haymaking today, and was I going to get people to put up the hay today? 'I'll get plenty of people on days when hay can't be put up.'

'Oh, take all of them,' he said, 'I don't need them today at all; but leave the cook.'

'Oh, we'll need a cook ourselves,' I said.

'Mistress Kane will cook for you,' he said. (She was his son's wife; she lived down there at Ross.) 'Are you taking a cart with you?'

'I am.'

'Well, don't go until you take them with you,' he said. 'And speak to the barmaid to see if she'll go there, and tell her that if she'll go, I'll do the bar for her, I'm getting up at once.'

I came down. The barmaid was a girl from Inverness called Lizzie MacKay. I asked her if she was willing to go to the hay, along with us.

'I'll surely do that,' she said, 'if I get to go there.'

'Oh, well then, he says to tell you that if you go, he'll do the bar for you, that he's getting up at once. He wants you to take plenty of food and everything with you.'

She began to fill a basket then, and I went to harness a cart, and I took all the servants with me. Kane had a fellow who used to go up to the top of Ben Lomond as a guide, with ponies, Rob Baird. I took him with me. When we arrived at Ross, the basket was sent in to William's wife, and she was asked to send out tea to them at ten o'clock. Then we began to scatter the haycocks and shake them out.[18] When it was about eleven o'clock we saw a puffer going up the loch; it was the puffer that used to bring coal to us. The other fellow said:

'My word, I see Peter's going up the loch there with the puffer, and he's steering for Rowardennan. I wouldn't say you won't have to go up to Rowardennan today yet.'

'Indeed, I won't have to,' I said. 'What would she have for Rowardennan?'

'Unless it's coal.'

'It isn't,' I said, 'they got their coal already.'

'Has she coal for the Lodge?' he said. There were two lodges to the north of us.

'She hasn't,' I said. 'The Lodge itself has got its coal.'

'Oh, I know that,' he said, 'but I heard the gamekeeper say that they were expecting a small quantity of Welsh coals for the yacht. Maybe that's what she's got.'

'Oh, well then,' I said, 'isn't William up there, hasn't he got a horse and cart, won't that give him a little exercise? There won't be much altogether.'

'Oh, I don't think there will,' he said.

Anyway, we went to our dinner. When we had had dinner, and came out, there was a lot of hay which had been pulled by sledge into mounds to be made into big stacks, in low places. I began to sledge in the hay and two big stacks were going up together, the work was going on just like a house on fire. But who the pity did I see appearing but William, coming without jacket or cap or anything but in his shirt sleeves. He came straight to me.

'You'll have to go up with that horse now,' he said, 'there's four tons of coal there to put out for Mr Mair at the Lodge.'

'Go and take yourself to John o' Groat's house,' I said. 'You've got a horse and cart up there—put the coal out or leave it aboard. How am I going to go up and leave everyone standing here, isn't it the horse that's keeping them working?'

'That horse won't put it out,' he said.

'That horse *will* put it out,' I said. 'I put out fifteen tons with him a fortnight ago.'

'He won't even put a ton out for you today.'

'What'll stop him?'

'Go along, I don't care anyway,' William said, 'whether you go or stay, but I'm off anyway.'

'You aren't going off,' I said, 'you stay and work the horse here, and I'll go up and put the coal out with the horse that's up there, since he couldn't take it with him.'

'You needn't trouble, unless you take the horse here.'

'And why,' I said, 'if the other horse couldn't do it, didn't you bring him down here when there's so much hay? You could have got this one.'

'I wasn't told to do that,' he said.

'You weren't told!' I said. 'You're always coming to me with your extraordinary orders. Go and unload it or else if you can't, put it out on the sea!'

'Go on then,' William said, 'you'll come back for him yet.'

I went off. I hadn't gone far when I was repenting that I hadn't taken the horse even though the day never came that he got the hay up, since the boss hadn't a horse that would unload coal. I knew he was very much frightened of wetting his feet in the water, he was a tramways horse and had never got his feet wet before.

When I got back to the hotel, I saw the boss coming out. He came over to the road to meet me.

'You've come,' he said.

'I have.'

'Did you bring the horse along?'

'I didn't. If I'd brought him, I might as well have brought everyone along, isn't it the horse that's keeping them working?'

'Oh, I didn't mean to trouble you at all,' he said. 'I know you've plenty to do where you are; when the puffer came I sent William with the black horse to unload the coal. It seems they couldn't get the horse into the water; there were six of them at it and Peter himself came off along with them at the end!'

'Well, that's terrible,' I said. 'I unloaded fifteen tons of coal with him a fortnight ago.'

'Oh, I know you did,' Kane said. 'I don't know what you'll do, but anyway the coal must be unloaded because I'm paid something every year for carting for the lodges, and if it isn't unloaded, it can be charged against me.'

'And why didn't William bring the horse down to me, he would have got the other one?'

'The bloody fool,' said Kane. 'I didn't remember to tell him that; couldn't he have had the sense to think of it himself?'

I went off down to the stable with the boss following me. The black horse was standing in the stall with his harness on. I turned him out. His head had been cut in two places where they had been hitting him with sticks. Well, I was glad to have that against them itself.

'Well,' I said, 'if they weren't able to work him, they might at least have left him whole. How can horse or man work if that's the way they're treated?'

'How can they?' Kane said, 'but what more do you expect of them? They didn't need to hurt him, if they couldn't get him into the water.'

'They've hurt him all right,' I said. 'Where's the cart?'

'William left the cart up at the Lodge, he only brought the horse down.'

I went off up with the horse, but when I got in sight of the puffer—the skipper's name was Peter—it wasn't a 'God bless me' I got when I appeared.

'Where are you going with that horse?' he said.

'Haven't I come to unload your coal?'

'You won't unload coal with that horse today!'

'He unloaded coal for you before.'

'If he did, he won't do it today. Are you going to do something six men couldn't do?'

'I don't know that you yourself wouldn't do something a dozen couldn't do,' I said.

'Whatever I'd do, you don't need to bother trying with that horse.'

'Take it easy!' I said. 'Keep your wig on! There's no proof like a trial.'[19]

He kept quiet then. I went and harnessed the horse to the cart, and went down to the loch with him. When he reached the loch he stuck out his four feet and began to back. I turned him round and backed him towards the loch. When his hind feet reached the loch, he stood there and wouldn't move. Then I jumped off the cart and caught hold of his head and began to lead him down beside the loch to try to get his feet wet. He only went sideways, neighing. I didn't know what in the world to do. I would sooner have drowned myself than gone back to get the horse I had left. Peter was striding to and fro on the deck.

'Isn't it a ploy for me,' he said, 'watching you playing with that horse! Devil take me if I don't let your boss see that it'll cost him plenty if I'm going to lie here under four tons of coal till Monday!'

'I don't care if you charge him a pound a minute,' I said. 'Why hadn't he horses that could unload coal?'

'He has that,' he said, 'if you'd brought them here.'

'That horse is working somewhere else,' I said.

'What the devil's you and your work to me?'

He wouldn't listen to me at all. But then I thought the horse might be taken out by the derrick.

'Have you got as much wire on that derrick,' I said, 'as will let the hook ashore to me here?'

'I've as much as would let it out to the Lodge.'

'All right, slacken your chain, I'll take him into the water with the derrick.'[20]

He went and slackened his chain. I just waded out to get the hook, and came in and put it right on the axle of the cart, and it was caught by the end. 'Heave on, steady now!'[20]

Peter began to tighten it. When I saw the strain coming on the wire, I let the horse have it around the ears with the willow switch! Out he went backwards until the water was up to his flanks. By then the water was coming into the box of the cart, and I couldn't manage to get the hook off the axle. The skipper turned to me then and said:

'What are you going to do now?'[20]

'Slack it ashore,'[20] I said.

He slackened it in then. Then I tried to back the horse back. He wouldn't. It was 'heave on' again.'[20] Then he paid it out again. When I saw that the axle was about to go under, I made him stop. Then I took the hook off the axle. This time the horse backed, and they put the coal over the side of the puffer [into the cart]. Then I got up on the trams and threw the reins to him and asked him to tie them. Half a ton of coal was put into the cart. Well, I only had to cope it just opposite us above the bank of the loch; the Lodge people would take it away from there. I came away with it, and coped it up above the bank of the loch; I jumped on to the cart, gave the horse the switch, and off he went down back to the loch. I turned him around and backed him to the puffer. He didn't refuse any more. I didn't take twenty minutes unloading the four tons of coal.

'Haven't you got your coal unloaded now?' I said.

'Oh, well, I have,' said Peter. 'I don't know who's the more obstinate, yourself or the horse!'

'Well, if I'm not to be his master, he isn't going to be mine, anyway,' I said.

'Will you be so good as to cast off the ropes?' Peter said.

'I'll cast off every rope you've got there.'

I went and cast off the ropes and let the puffer get away. The staff of the Lodge, the gamekeeper and the gardener and the forester and the ghillie, were at their tea at the time; I was by myself. I went back to the steading and unyoked the cart, and put the horse into the stable, and I was looking out to see if I could get into the bothy without anyone seeing me so as I could change into dry clothes. I went through the garden and got to the bothy; I didn't see anyone outside. I threw off my wet clothes and put on dry ones. I was then ready, I wasn't going to go into the hotel at all; I went out, and who was coming out of the kitchen door but Mr Kane with a tray and a carving knife on his way to the meat safe to cut some meat. He stopped in the doorway.

'Hello!' he said. 'So you've arrived?'

'I have,' I said.

'Did you unload the coal?'

'I did.'

'What the devil are you saying? Was anyone with you?'

'I didn't see anyone but Peter.'

'Are you saying you've done what six men couldn't do?'

'Well, I don't know,' I said. 'I don't think that one man should have failed to do it, let alone six, for four tons of coal.'

'Well, well, well, well,' he said, 'I never heard the like, well I never in all my born days.'[21] He went and put the tray on the window-sill outside. 'Come in this way, Angus, and follow me.'[22]

I went in after him. He went in and went to the bar. He turned round. 'What are you going to have?' he said.

'Oh, I'll take a glass of beer,' I said.

'Oh, hell with you! You'll get plenty of water at the back of the kitchen!'

'Oh, you'll get plenty of water in Loch Lomond too,' I said.

'Yes; you'll take a glass of good Irish whisky'll no do you any harm.'

'All right, sir, I'll take anything.'[23]

He went and bent down below the counter and took out a bottle. There was one of the big tumblers from the coffee-room on the counter; it would hold just a pint. Kane took out the cork and caught hold of the bottle and held it over the tumbler. I called, 'Stop! Stop! Stop!' He didn't stop until he had filled it on the counter to the last drop.

'Oh, heavens!' I said, 'that's too much of a good thing, I'm not going to take that!'

'Not at all. Any Hielandman that wouldn't drink that wasn't worth a damn. Throw it below the bonnet!'[24]

There was nothing else for it. Well, I took half of it; but it wouldn't do, I had to take every drop of it. I said to myself I'll not get out of the door, I'll be done for—but I'll fall down indoors! Then Kane turned to me and asked me if I was going down to Ross again.

'I am,' I said, 'or else Ross'll be like the coal.'

'There's nothing more certain,' he said. 'But go along to the kitchen and get a cup of tea before you go.'

'Oh, you don't need to be bothering,' I said, 'I'll manage as I am.'

'It's no bother at all.' He called to the cook. 'Get a cup of tea ready for Angus,'[25] he said.

She answered then that the tea was ready. 'Come in,' she said. I went along. Kane came, and took a plate, and went out. In a moment he came back, with a pile of roast meat cut into slices.

'Here,' he said, 'take this with your tea. He unloaded the coal,' he said, 'with the horse which six men couldn't work, and my great big son along with them; well I never in all my born days!'[26]

He went off. By then I was bursting with laughter.

I didn't care what happened so long as I got outside without falling down! I got out, and went down the road, laughing to myself like a half-wit. I was able to stand all right, but when I began to walk, my legs were getting in each other's way! Eventually I got down where they were at work. I went over to William, who was sledging the hay.

'You've come back now,' he said, 'worse than you left.' They had seen the puffer going past, and they thought that she had taken the coal with her.

'I don't think so,' I said.

'You weren't able to unload the coal.'

'Nobody says so but you.'

'Oh, Peter wasn't going to stay till you chose to arrive with a horse that would unload his coal at all,' he said.

'Peter stayed till he was clear.'

The other fellow came up. 'Did you unload it, Angus?' he asked.

'I did,' I said.

'Here, that's better than a pound!' he said. 'Pay up your bet, William.' He and William had had a bet on it. He had bet William ten shillings that I would unload it as sure as I had gone.

'I won't,' said William, 'but you will! The devil didn't unload a pound of coal; if he did, he didn't do it with the black horse!'

'If I didn't, I didn't do it with the white one,' I said. 'I didn't care what colour he was, white or black.'

'You'll have to pay the bet,' said the other fellow.

'I'll pay it if he unloaded it with the black horse.'

'Isn't the horse itself here?'

'Oh yes, but time will tell.'[27]

'Indeed, you haven't done much since I left,' I said. 'You could have put up more hay than this. But you won't get away from here until the last stack is up, though they were going to church tomorrow before you were finished.'

Then I began sledging the hay, and William was put to forking. Just when the sun was setting, we had finished the last stack of it. I was never more pleased in my life, I had got the hay up, and I had got the coal unloaded. They packed on to the cart then, and when we arrived at the hotel, the Lodge people were there, the gamekeeper and his boss were there. When William saw him, he jumped off the cart and went over to the gamekeeper.

'Did Angus unload the coal with the black horse?' he asked.

'We don't know what horse he had; we had gone to our tea, and when we came out, the puffer had gone, and we thought she had taken the coal with her; when we went down, the coal was outside there.'

'Are you sure it wasn't Kennedy's horse he had?' asked William. (Kennedy was working felling timber above us.)

'It wasn't, indeed,' said the gamekeeper. 'That horse was up on the Ptarmigan for the last three days.'

William was done for then, he didn't know what to say.

They went into the tap-room; who came around but the boss!

'There you are,' he said. 'Six heroes! Aren't you ashamed? My only Highlander has beaten the lot of you today! Aren't you ashamed!'

They would sooner have had sticks taken to them than be listening to him! William had no doubt whatever that I hadn't used witchcraft, that that wasn't the way I had got the horse out! And that's how I left them.

III

The Cask of Paraffin

Once when I had been down at Ross, it was late before I came back. William met me outside the hotel, and said:

'You'd better keep on down to the pier, Angus, since you've got the cart ready, there's a barrel of paraffin on the pier that came this afternoon, and I didn't get to bring it up. There isn't a drop in the house, they're just waiting for you, they've only got candles.'

'Didn't you have a horse and cart here since early morning, why didn't you bring up the barrel?'

'I hadn't anyone to help me put it on the cart.'

'Couldn't you put it on the cart yourself?'

'I couldn't have, nor could you!'

'What would stop you?'

'I'll bet you five shillings you won't put it on the cart by yourself!'

'All right, it's on. Go on home now!'

'Off you go, then,' he said.

I went off and kept on down to the pier; it was a wooden pier. In the summertime the loch used to be very low. One day when I was down at the pier I had been looking to see the best plan I might make to put casks into the cart by myself. Casks of beer used to come, and I'd have no one to help me put them out. There was a bank at the end of the pier, above the loch, and there was a place cut out there where the carts could go up; we used to be taking gravel there for the paths.

Well, I said to myself that that was a good place, if the casks were rolled up off the pier to the bank there, I'd only have to bring the cart in below, and the casks would roll into it by themselves. I arrived at the pier, and rolled the cask up to the cart, I got the cart in below, and there was nothing to getting the cask into it. I went up to the hotel with it and came round by the back. When William heard the cart coming round, he came out. Then I took the cask out of the cart, and kicked it along. 'Here's your cask now,' I said, 'pay up your bet.'

'Ah, well,' he said, 'it looks as if the devil will do anything for you.'

'Isn't it a good thing I've got such command over him,' I said. 'It's the other way round with you!'

He didn't know how on earth I had got the cask into the cart. There wasn't a plank on the pier, or anything to put it in with; he was asking the gamekeeper next day if there had been anyone on the pier late yesterday; there hadn't been, they hadn't seen anyone on the pier. But he paid me the five shillings!

How I Shot the Blackcock

One morning when I was in the stable, what did I see but a blackcock sitting in the middle of the field in front of the stable. My word, I was blessing myself, and the sun was rising. There was a lad with me looking after the cattle, called Johnny MacLaren. I called to Johnny to go along and get the gun, which was in the scullery.

'Off with you and bring me the gun, and two cartridges. It's in the scullery.'

He went off. He came back with the gun behind him. The blackcock was preening itself right in the middle of the field. I looked; I couldn't manage to hit him from the stable, he was a long way away from me. But there was an oak tree growing in the field, and I thought that if I could get the oak between him and myself, I might manage it. I rushed out of the stable door and got to the ditch beside the main road, and kept along the ditch until I got the oak-tree between myself and the blackcock. Then I went through the fence, and got to behind the tree. I cocked both barrels and fired the first, and hit him with the first shot, but no quicker did he fall than he got up again. He didn't move when I tried the second barrel; he fell dead at the edge of the loch.

I made for the stable as quick as I ever did; I went into it and left the gun. There was a wheelbarrow full of manure in the stable. I took hold of it and went out with it. When I went out, I saw the gamekeeper standing at the end of the house just as he had jumped out of bed. (The gamekeeper's house was only a short way away from me.) I stood looking here and there to see if I could see who had fired the shot!

Then I went back into the stable with the wheelbarrow. When we had swept out the stable and cleaned the horses, I said to Johnny MacLaren:

'Off with you now, take a sack, and go down round and put him in it, go around, don't come straight up to the house at all. Go round the point until you get to the other side of the hotel.'

He went off, and found the blackcock dead at the edge of the loch. That evening I saw the gamekeeper down at the pier. He came over to me.

'Who on earth,' he said, 'who fired those two shots in the morning today?'

'I don't know,' I said, 'unless you fired them yourself.'

'Not me,' he said, 'I hadn't got up when I heard them.'

'I was in the stable,' I said. 'I came out, you yourself were at the end of the house; I thought that you had fired them.'

'I certainly didn't,' he said. 'But indeed, they weren't far away.'

'Indeed, they weren't far away at all,' I said. 'I didn't see anyone moving but yourself.'

He didn't succeed in finding out who had killed the black-cock!

The Drink Trade

When the Glasgow Fair holidays were on, trippers used to come out to Rowardennan; sometimes as many as eight hundred came out on the steamer, to climb Ben Lomond. Well, the day before they came—the boss knew the day they were coming—he used to make us draw water from a pump a bit away from the hotel, the piped water wouldn't do, and put it in a hogshead in the cellar. We would fill the hogshead half-way up, and he would come out then with a pint stoup, and I don't know what the stuff was, but he used to pour it into the hogshead. A little later he would come out with a stick, and stir up the contents of the hogshead thoroughly. The next day, they would bring it in and put it into bottles and into a cask, and that was sold for whisky! I don't know how the people who were drinking it survived; when I saw this, it put me off every whisky I ever had seen!

That wasn't what surprised me most, but hearing people praising it, saying it was good. It was a long, long way from being good. That's the way the boss was carrying on a lot of his enterprises.

I saw him do something very odd and very bad. There were men working in the woods, felling trees, and on this night, a Saturday night, they were in the hotel. While I was in the kitchen at supper-time, the bell sounded down in the taproom. I heard the boss come down the passage. He shouted was I there, 'Are you there, Angus?' I answered and said I was.

'Will you answer that bell for me?' he said.

I got up and went along. There they were; they ordered a round of drinks, a glass of whisky and a pint of beer each. I went back and got it for them. It was getting near to ten o'clock. One of them turned to me and said:

'Go and bring me a bottle of whisky.'

I went off down to the bar. I said the man wanted a bottle of whisky. Kane went and handed over a bottle. The cheapest whisky cost three shillings a bottle; there was another brand at four shillings, and one at four and six. It was a three-shilling one I got. I came back with it and handed it over.

'What's this?' the man said.

'Three shillings,' I replied.

'Oh, it was "spirit"[28] I wanted.'

'Why didn't you say that before?' I said.

I went off back to the bar with it, and put it on the counter.

'Wouldn't he have it at all?' said Kane.

'Oh yes, but it's "spirit" that he wants.'

'Oh, indeed,' said Kane. He went and opened a drawer and took out a label, and stuck it on the side of the bottle. 'Charge him four and six!'

I had to go back with the bottle; and I was sore at heart taking four and six for the very same bottle! That's the way a lot of things used to be done in public houses, you wouldn't need to pay heed to a label, whether it was white or black or brown!

The Time the Cellar was Cleared Out

There was an old cellar at Rowardennan. The boss was going to pull it down and build a new one outside apart from the hotel. Anyway, one Saturday the slaters were taking the roof off the old cellar. There was drink in it, and we were never in such a hurry as we were taking the drink out of it and bringing it into the coffee-room. There were bottles in lockers all around the cellar. Well, all the lockers that had been emptied were left open. The slaters were on the roof, and pieces of slate and wood were falling around our heads while we were carrying the bottles into the coffee-room.

By nightfall we had finished, and the slaters had finished taking off the roof. On Sunday the boss's son William and I went out to the ruin, which was full of rubbish. I noticed that one of the lockers was closed; every one that had been emptied had been left open. This one was low down. I went and opened it and cleared it out. It was full of bottles covered with mildew, so long was it since they had been put there. The labels were off the bottles.

'By God, look here!' I said.

'Ah! take every one of them, take every one of them!' said William.

'Get out of my sight, you sprig of damnation!' I said.

'I'll do that,' said William, as he began to grab the bottles and thrust them into his coat, and into his pockets, until at last he was as round as a barrel! He went off down to the stable. I didn't know what in the world I should say, but I went and took an armful of bottles into the bar to the boss. The boss couldn't think what it was.

'Look at this,' I said, 'there was a locker which we forgot to open yesterday.'

'Oh, what a good thing the masons didn't see it,' he said.

My word, I said to myself that someone just as bad as the masons had seen it! I took two dozen bottles in to Kane, and I'm sure his son William took away another dozen, every one of them. 'Never mind,' said William—I don't know where he hid them—'Never mind. You won't get a drop; you could have had plenty yourself.'

'I don't want a drop of it,' I said. 'Away with it out of my sight.'

William took the bottles home after dark. That's the way he used to carry on!

How I Got the Big Irishman to Leave the Bar

I remember how one night the woodcutters were up at the hotel. Most of them were Irishmen; they were working for Mr Kennedy the wood merchant, who had bought the wood up there. He had a big squad working at it, and that night, a Saturday night, they were up at the hotel, drinking. There was one Irishman there called O'Connell, and his appearance was just fearful. His neck was as thick as a bull's. He and the Boots fell out. It was after ten o'clock, and the Boots was telling them to go out, and out they would not go.

Then the boss came up and called to us to go and kick them out. They were standing in the passage, the boss's own son, the Boots, and the waiters, and my word, I was frightened to go down in case it happened that I got a blow that would knock out my brains.

'Wait there where you are,' I said, 'and I'll go down to them.'

I went along. The Irishman was standing with his jacket off. Then I opened the door.

'Have you come to put me out?' he said.

'No, indeed,' I said, 'I'd like to see the man who'd put you out.'

'There isn't anyone who'll put a hand on me; that's the way he'll go, out through the window!'

'Oh well,' I said, 'if you killed us tonight I know you'd be sorry enough for it tomorrow; but can I be of any help to you?'

'I don't know,' he said. 'I asked for a bottle of whisky.'

'What a pity you didn't ask me for it a quarter of an hour ago.'

'It's an hour since I asked for it, and I never got it yet.'

'Well,' I said, 'it isn't the proprietor who's to blame for that at all; it's the fault of the fellow who was waiting on you.'

'I don't care who's to blame; I won't go out until I get what I asked for.'

'Well, I know it isn't for tonight that you're wanting it, that it's for your "morning", isn't it?'

'It is,' he said.

'Well, you go home tonight, then,' I said, 'and come up tomorrow at eight o'clock, and I'll get it for you; I can't do better for you than that.'

'Will you keep your word?'

'By the Book, I'll keep my word any day,' I said.

He caught hold of his jacket and put it on. 'Get out of here, boys,' he said. Out by the door he went. I went out and closed the door and bade them good-bye. When I came back, the bullies were awaiting me in the passage.

'Well, indeed,' I said, 'I think that it looks as if you were drunk and not those men. I'm thinking that it wouldn't cost much to be polite to them, after they've been spending their money.'

'Oh,' said the boss, 'Angus is the boy for them.'[29]

On Sunday morning I was in the stable. When I was about to come along for my breakfast, I look and oh! for pity's sake who did I see coming up the road but the Irishman! looking the worse for wear.[30] I stopped until he arrived.

'Have you got what you promised me last night?' he said.

'Not yet,' I said, 'come here.'

I went and opened the bothy door.

'You sit there until I come out.'

I went in. It was a girl from Inverness who was working in the bar. I went in to see the barmaid.

'Oh, heavens, Lizzie,' I said, 'see and give me a bottle of whisky, I promised one to the Irishman last night, to get them away in peace.'

'For goodness sake, then, see that no one finds it out.'

'Neither God nor man will find it out,' I said. 'You go ahead.'

She went and handed me the bottle. I came out and handed it to the Irishman.

'There it is, now,' I said.

Oh, my dear, he stood up! He wanted me to take a share

of it right off! 'I won't take a drop of it now, in case they notice the smell of it on me indoors, I'm going in to my breakfast. I'll take a dram from you some time. Off you go!'

I got clear of the Irishman, and I was pleased enough that a row didn't start on account of that other rascal, he was to blame, the Boots!

The Man Who Went Wrong in the Head

Mr Kane had a waiter who came from Shetland, a very nice lad; and what did he do but go off his head. The first time he was noticed was before sunrise outside at the front door, with a towel tied round his head. He was standing up to his work right enough but he was terribly quiet, compared to what he usually was. The boss went and sent for the doctor and the doctor came on Sunday with another man along with him. There was a wooden porch[31] in front of the hotel, which was a smoking-room for the gentry. The boss met the doctor outside, and took him into this smoking-room, and was telling him how the waiter was standing up to his work all right, but that there was something wrong with him.

'Go and send him in to us here with a refreshment,' said the doctor.

The boss went out. The waiter was working about the house. Kane said to him, 'There are two gentlemen there out in the smoking-room, asking for a refreshment. Go and take two glasses out to each of them.'

The waiter went off the moment he had got them, and went out. The doctor started talking to him when he came out, and began to praise the place, how pretty it was—it was a pretty place and it was no wonder that tourists were coming there.

'Oh, it isn't, it isn't,' the waiter said. 'It's a bad place! A dirty place! A terribly dirty place! An ugly place!'

'What! it's not,' said the doctor. 'This isn't dirty, this is a fine place!'

'Look up there! there's nothing but cobwebs,' said the waiter.

'Tut! that's nothing. I used to know an hotel in Ireland and the name it was called was the Cobwebs Hotel.'

Oh, the waiter rushed out of the door when he heard this. The boss came out then, he had been inside.

'What do you think about him now?' he said.

'Oh well,' said the doctor, 'don't oppose him in any way; the sooner you get him away the better. Don't oppose him at all.'

But that night—I wasn't thinking anything of it, though I was finding him silent like this—I was sleeping in a bothy outside, with two others, all the summer and autumn; it was in the hotel that I used to sleep all winter and spring. I had to attend to the ferry, it didn't matter whether anyone came by night or by day, if I could get across, I had to go. It was a 'Queen's ferry'.

We had gone to bed. I hadn't closed the door of the bothy, but I had pushed it to. I was just falling asleep when I heard the door being opened, and the waiter shouted: 'Are you there, Angus?'[32]

I lifted my head and said I was.

'Oh,' he said, 'I thought you were over the ferry.'

'Get along with you, you and your ferry at this time of the night,' I said, when I saw who was there. He went back outside without saying a word.

The kitchen door had a wire spring on it, and would close by itself, and would give a blow when it closed. I had my ear lifted to see if I could hear if he went in by the kitchen door, when I was going to get up and lock the bothy door. I didn't hear anything. I was afraid to get up, naked as I was, I was afraid he would catch me at the door, that he was only standing beside the door. But in a minute he came running, and he came over to the bed and put his hands on the bed above me. I was pretending I was fast asleep! Then he went back outside and came in with a white sheet, and spread it on top of me on the bed. Then he ran off back and it wasn't long before he came with a bunch of flowers, and began to put the flowers around my head and my feet, and he put a bunch of them on my chest. I lay still half dead with fright! Then he ran out again and I heard the clink of a bucket outside. What was it but an old zinc bucket that came one time with soft soap. It would hold four gallons. It was as full of holes as a sieve;

it had been lying beside the wall outside. I heard him dipping it in a trough of water that was behind the kitchen and in he ran with it and you could hear the noise in the bucket with water streaming through its sides. He set it down in front of the bed and out he went.

But I was terrified that he was going to put me in the bucket and I jumped out of bed and caught hold of it and threw it after him. I was at the door and locked it. After a moment he came to the door and tried it, and the door was locked. Then he went to the window, and put his hands to the window. He was looking in. I made the others get up and get dressed, not knowing what he mightn't do. They got up and we got dressed. He was all night back and forth in and out of the house. What had he done but put a catch on the kitchen door, it was ajar,[33] it wasn't closing at all, he was free to go in and out through the house.

Well, the next day his sister who was living in Glasgow came, the boss sent her a telegram, and she came on account of it to get him. He went away with her and I never heard what became of him afterwards.

The Ghost in Room Number Thirteen

One night, we were playing cards in the kitchen. The house-maid was a girl from Islay. We heard one of the bells ringing down in the lobby. She didn't move. I said to her, 'There's a call for you, Janet!'

'It isn't,' she said.

'It must be. Isn't the bell ringing?'

'Oh, there's nobody there,' she said.

A minute after, the bell rang again, and the house resounded to it. I got up and went along taking a candle that was on the table, and she got up along with me. The bell was ringing unceasingly; it was number thirteen upstairs.

'Isn't there someone there now?' I said.

'There isn't.'

'Where's the traveller?'

'In number five on the ground floor.'

'Go on up,' I said. 'There must be someone there.'

'I won,t,' she said, 'not even for all of Scotland.'

'Will you come up if I go up?'

'I will.'

'Come along, then.'

I went off up the stairs. When I was at the top of the stairs, I heard walking in the room just as clear as if there was someone in it.

'Knock on the door.'

She wouldn't go near the door, but clutched hold of me. I turned the handle and opened the door. There was no one there, but I heard a buzz as if a bee were going out of the room above my head. I thought I ought to find someone there anyway; I looked in the wardrobe that was in the room, and there was no one; I looked under the bed; no one.

'Oh, well, my God,' she said, 'haven't you got a nerve!'

'It looks as if the Devil were paying a visit here, anyway!'

I went downstairs. A week afterwards I was asleep in the bothy outside—it was there I used to sleep all summer and autumn; in the winter and spring I used to sleep in the hotel. I heard just the same thing, a noise[34] in the loft above my bed, and I thought that the house had fallen down. I jumped out of bed, I heard the wood creaking[35] after I had got out of bed. I lit a candle, and looked into the loft above, and didn't see anything, there was nothing in the loft. Well, I said to myself that something extraordinary must have fallen above. When I got up in the morning the first turn I did was to go up to the loft to see what had fallen. There was not as much as a stick in the loft! I was saying to myself that there must be something accursed there.

There were two other fellows sleeping in the bothy along with me, they were there and they heard it themselves and they didn't move, the bedclothes were over their heads! But a week later, they were talking about ghosts—we were indoors in the kitchen—about how they were seeing something a mile down from the hotel, at a place called Callwood.

'Well, I don't think you need to go as far as Callwood to find a ghost, wasn't there one in the bothy a few nights ago?'

'My word,' said the other fellow, 'did you hear it?'

'I heard it,' I said. 'Did you?'

'By Mary, I did, I was too frightened to take the bed-clothes off my head.'

'Well, I got up,' I said, 'and lit a candle. I didn't see anything.'

And that's all the ghosts I ever saw or heard!

The Time I Took William and Wife for a Sail

Once I went as a gentleman along with William Kane, the hotelkeeper's son, and some of the maids; they were bargaining with me all the autumn to give them a sail, and I was promising I would, but indeed I didn't expect to. Anyway one Saturday at the end of autumn every one of the visitors had left the hotel, there wasn't anyone in it. When I was at my supper who came in but the hotelkeeper's son, William.

'Well, it's time for you to go to bed, tomorrow's the day of the sail, you'll have to get up pretty early.'

'I won't get up any earlier tomorrow than I usually do,' I said; 'surely you've plenty of time to go for a sail after your dinner?'

'Who's going to go then? No, we'll go at eight o'clock in the morning.'

'If you do, I won't go with you! Anyone who likes can!'

'Well, it's a poor thing for you to be promising a sail when you won't give it to us at all.'

He went off home. But when I was coming out of the stable on Sunday morning, who on earth was coming dressed up all ready to set off but William and his wife.

'God bless me!' he said, 'are you still here unwashed and unshaven?'

'Oh, be off with you to John o' Groat's,' I said.

'Hurry up!'

I went to my breakfast. Then William came out. The boss had a boat which wasn't to be given out to anyone at all except a lady and a gentleman when he said so himself. But she was the one he used himself when he was going up and down the loch; it was the one he used to take. It was a very attractive boat, a real pleasure boat, it had sails, it was more than twenty feet long. I went into the bothy when I had had my breakfast and began to shave. William arrived.

'Where's the sails of yon boat?' he said.

'What boat?'

'That pleasure boat.'

'There are plenty of boats,' I said. 'Don't you know very well that that one isn't go to out with anyone until himself asks for it to be let out?'

'Can't you take any boat you want to?'

'Oh, that's all right for you to say,' I said, 'but, anyway, I'm not going to take that one unless I'm told to.'

'What one are you going to take? Who on earth's going to be rowing up there; what a sail that would be!'

'Well, won't you take the fishing boat? It's got a sail.'

'Ah! it's some boat!' said William, turning away.

'Go on in to your father, then,' I said. 'I don't care if he gives you a yacht, I'll sail it.'

'I won't!'

He wouldn't need to! If he went in to see him, he would tell him to go to hell! But then the maids came, and this was harder for me than William.

Tut, dear me, won't you give us a sail; it's a small thing; you aren't a gentleman every day of your life; what does he know about it?'

'Ho, he doesn't know right enough,' I said, 'but he might know sometime. Get out of my sight then,' I said, 'her sails are in the store, down at the pier.'

William went off then. Then he came back again. Where are the cushions for the seats?'

'Oh, get to hell out of here, you and your cushions. They're in the machine's shed; can't you manage at all without cushions?'

He went off at that. He came back three times to hurry me up. Then I went down; they got on board.

'Which way do you want to go? Up or down?'

'Up to Tarbet.' That was five miles to the north of us.

The sails were hoisted and sure enough we had a fair south wind right to Tarbet. We arrived at Tarbet and they landed there, and went up the pier. There was a fellow from Benbecula in charge of the pier at Tarbet; he was living in the Tarbet Hotel.

'Who are the tourists you've got today?' he said, coming over to me.

'Ho!' I said, 'some of the maids and Kane's own son.'

Everyone would recognize him.

'Is that his wife who's along with you there?'

'It is,' I said.

'My word,' he said, 'isn't she coarse-looking!'

'She is,' I said, 'and she's coarse in lots of other ways too.'

The party stopped at the top end of the pier waiting for me; then William shouted for me to hurry.

'See and keep an eye on the boat,' I said. 'I must go off with them there.'

'Oh, there's no fear for the boat,' said the Benbecula man.

I went off up; we went into the hotel there; then we ordered lunch; you could get a dram if you wanted to, on Sunday. When we had had our lunch, what did William do then but order a conveyance over to Loch Long, to Arrochar and Tarbet. We went off then to Arrochar and Tarbet, and they went into the inn there. Oh, then the weather was getting overcast and the wind was rising and it looked like rain. My word, I was on tenterhooks that the sails and the cushions and everything would get wet, and I was asking William to leave, and he wouldn't, we were early enough! He ordered dinner for us here in the Tarbet hotel, it was early enough to be there at dinner-time, at seven o'clock!

My word, I repented of having come! But, anyway, it happened that it began to rain. Then we came over, and as soon as I arrived with the trap to the hotel I kept on down to the pier. Who met me but the Benbecula man, the fellow who was in charge of the pier.

'Where are you going?'

'I'm going to look at the boat.'

'Oh, you don't need to,' he said. 'I've taken her up behind the pier, and taken out the sails and the cushions, they're in the store. You needn't be thinking of going down tonight with her,' he said. It had become extremely rough.

'I'm sure I don't,' I said. 'I believe the boat would make it all right.'

'Oh, she would,' he said, 'if the ones with you were like yourself, but—how's William?'

'Just a hopeless case there,' I said.

'Oh, indeed, I wouldn't advise you to go with the crew you've got,' he said.

'No more would I do it. I'll walk to the ferry.' There was a ferry between Rowardennan and the other side. Anyway, we went in for our dinner. Indeed I didn't want it very much. When I had had my dinner, everything was harassing me,[36] I came out.

'Well,' I said, 'all you can do now is to walk to the ferry or else stay where you are. I'm going, anyway.'

'We're going too. Who the devil's going to walk to yon ferry? Aren't you a hardy one?[37] Take it easy!' They went back. The trap was ordered out again to take us to the ferry. The driver turned out again. We reached the ferry. It was a man called Robertson who had the inn at Inverbeg, opposite Rowardennan. He met us there.

'Where have you come from like this?' he said.

'I've come down from Tarbet.'

'Was it your boat I saw going up in the morning?'

'It was,' I said. 'I had to leave her at Tarbet. William is blind drunk and I haven't anyone to help me.' He began to laugh. 'Will you go out with them again?' he said.

'Not in this world,' I said. 'Where's the ferryman?'

'In the kitchen.'

'See and get him out, that he'll put us across.'

'It's pretty rough,' he said.

'What! rough!' I said. 'I'd go across yet.'

Robertson asked a lad who was there to go in and look for the ferryman. The lad went in. The ferryman came out.

'You'd better take these people across,' said Robertson.

'Oh, I don't care to, it's too rough.'

'Angus says he'd go across yet.'

'Oh, that's Angus himself.'

'Och, what's stopping you going over? I'll row over myself

along with you,' I said. 'It'll be easy for you to come back with her, she'll almost come back by herself.'

'They'll be wet,' he said.

'I don't care if they're as wet as seals,' I said.

Then they came and we went down to the boat, and went off in her. Upon my soul they were pretty wet before we got across! The boat wasn't keeping out a drop, she was only a small boat anyway. We reached the other side and when we arrived, William and his wife made for their house, and didn't come in (to the hotel) at all. The maids went in, streaming wet; the boss was delighted that they had been soaked!

But then on Monday morning, I had to go to the pier to meet the first steamer at nine o'clock. There were pier dues to be collected there, two pennies from everyone who came off the steamer. I went into the bar. The bag had been taken out of the bar, and I took hold of the bag, though the boss was there. He turned to me.

'Look here, Angus,' he said, 'I've got a telegram from the lady and gentleman, they're coming with the ten o'clock boat; they're good sorts, Angus; they were here last year. They're wanting that pleasure boat to be ready for them at the pier.'[38]

Aye! I didn't know where in the world I was standing! The boat at Tarbet! Get along now! I went out without saying a word. William was standing outside the bothy.

'Get along now, you devil!' I said, 'and get the boat you left at Tarbet last night, there's a lady and gentleman wanting her to be ready for them here at ten o'clock.'

'Did you tell the boss she was in Tarbet?'

'No, I didn't,' I said, 'what good would it do me to——'

'Huh! you didn't tell him. Isn't it all right,' he said. 'You go up now and Captain MacFarlane will bring it down behind the steamer.' He was the captain of the boat that was due at ten o'clock, she was then going down to Balloch.

'He won't,' I said. 'He won't tow it behind the steamer. She'll sink it.'

'If she does, try it up on board.'

'If he takes it, it won't be for nothing,' I said. 'I'm not going to pay the freight charge for it. Off you go; your father might be calling for me in a moment and no one knowing where I am. Though you were gone all day no one will ask where you are.'

Devil a step would he go to get her. I didn't know what in the world I should do.

'I won't go up near the hotel until you come,' he said. 'You won't be away long anyway.'

I went up to Tarbet with the steamer. When I got off, the good fellow from Benbecula was on the pier.

'Is it the boat you're wanting?' he said.

'Yes,' I said. 'Do you think MacFarlane will take it down behind the steamer?'

'Oh, yes, I think he will,' he said. 'If he doesn't he'll take it down on deck. You'll have to be at him as soon as he comes into the pier. He hasn't much time but while he's landing passengers and taking them on board.'

The other steamer was just leaving Inversnaid on the opposite side of the loch. The moment she came in beside the pier, I jumped in on the paddle-box and went to see the captain.

'Hello!' he said. 'Are you here today?'

'Yes,' I said, 'and I've a boat here today, will you manage to take it behind the steamer? I went out yesterday to give the maids and William and his wife a sail. William got drunk, and I had to leave the boat here. The boss doesn't know it's here at all. The folk who are asking for it at ten o'clock are aboard; and if the boss knew about it, I'd get the sack.'

He began to laugh. 'Where is it?' he said.

'Behind the pier there.'

'Bring it up here beside the steamer,' he said. 'We can't tow it behind us at all; I'll take it on board.'

I jumped into the boat and it was heaved up beside the steamer, and in a moment the captain told two of the lads to go down and put a sling on it. It was lifted up and let down on the deck, just beside the rail. When we arrived at Rowardennan it was lifted over the rail and I jumped into it, and untied the sling, and went over to a stone quay that was there, beyond the steamer pier. I raised the mast, and began to put the sails in order; I was just ready to come out of her, when the gentleman and the lady were coming towards me, along with William.

'Is the boat ready?' said the gentleman.

'It's fine and ready. Do you want a boatman?'

'Oh, no,' he said. 'We'll be in in two hours.'

'Oh, very good,' I said. I went off up to the hotel and went into the bar.

'Did the gentleman and the lady arrive?' asked the boss.

'They did,' I said. 'They're out with the boat.'

'When did they say they'd be in?'

'They said they'd be in in two hours.'

'See and watch them when they're coming in,' he said.

He never found out that the boat had been away. If he had, I would have been sent to John o' Groat's on account of William! But that day I swore that I would never take her out again to give a sail to any of them! That's what happened to me the day I went off as a gentleman and I would have been much better off if I had stayed indoors!

William and the Apparitions

William, the son of the farmer for whom I worked, wasn't of the best kind—he was a terrible drunkard. On this occasion I understand that he kept at it too long, and he went a bit wrong in the head with it. It was first noticed at dinner-time. He was asleep on a sofa, and his father went to awaken him for dinner, and when his father woke him, he turned on his father first. He was put in the parlour then, and a bed was put for him there, so that none of the tourists who were staying in the hotel might see him, or else no one would have stayed there but himself. And I had to go along with him.

I went in with William, and I had only just sat down on a chair there, and he had only just stretched himself out in the bed when he started to see the devil coming out from under the bed with two horns on. He was going to take off; he wasn't going to stay there any longer. I got a stick and sat in the chair, and every time I saw William get up and start to get out of the bed, I would aim a blow at the carpet in front of the bed, to try to hit the fellow with the horns who was coming out! I would tell him:

'Lie down now, don't be afraid, I won't let anything get at you, never mind what you see, try to go to sleep!'

Oh, he would be all right, if the fellow with the horns would only stay away.

'Never mind whether he goes or stays, I won't let him near you. Amn't I here guarding you? Go to sleep now!'

I would put the bedclothes around him. Then he would suddenly jump up, and begin to roll up the sheet, there was a snake in the sheet! I would jump up then and take hold of the sheet and spread it out. 'Look at that now, there's no snake nor anything else there. It was only something you imagined!'

'It was not; you've let it get away, you've let it get away!'

'Very well, let it be away.'

I would get him back into bed again and put the bedclothes in order. No sooner had he lain down than the fellow with the horns was coming out from under the bed! I was kept at it like this. When I had to go to the kitchen for a cup of tea, two other men had to come to relieve me, and many a time I had to leave it, and go down to be with him, he would pay no heed to them, he would knock them through the wall, but indeed he wouldn't lift his hand to strike me! I was three nights without a wink of sleep kept at it like this, and he didn't sleep either. I was sitting on a chair and however it happened, I dozed, and when I jumped up and opened my eyes, William was not in the bed. I nearly passed away for fear that he had done away with himself.

I ran down to the front door, and tried it, and found it locked. I went to the kitchen door, and that was locked. I returned and began to look at the windows to see if any of them had been raised or broken; none were. When I was going past the door of the coffee-room I noticed it wasn't closed at all, and I went and pushed it and went in. There was moonlight, and William was there sitting on one of the tables with nothing on but his nightshirt, looking at the window, trembling. I went over to him.

'My God, what are you doing there?'

'Hush, hush, hush, look at the men outside there, outside of the window!' I think it was the shadow of a branch of the tree opposite the window he was seeing, it was moving, and its shadow could be seen on the ground.

'Oh, yes,' I said, 'but if they see us here they'll come in through the window. You come out of there, let's get into the room.'

He came away from the table, and jumped three yards across the floor, and with three leaps he was back in bed, he couldn't stand on the floor for the 'clocks', big black beetles that used to be in houses, he was seeing them. Then I went and put him into bed. When he had been got into bed I said:

'Rest there, you'll be all right, whatever you see or notice don't mind, amn't I here to watch you?'

He laid his head upon the pillow. 'Oh, look at the dogs going up and down the chimney!'

'Yes,' I said, 'I'll make them stay up.' I went and poked the fire.

'Oh, see the little devil putting pins in my feet!' I began to strike the bed. 'I'll see to it that he won't stick a pin in anyone as long as he lives.' Then I beat off the little fellow. William sat upright in the bed.

'Oh, God, see the big ship! She was going to be on top of us!'

'Don't be afraid,' I said, 'don't be afraid!'

'Ah, she was going to be on top of us! Starboard! Yes! Look at that! She's gone by! Ah, well, you're a lad, Angus! She's gone by!'

After a short time: 'Oh, God, look at the sheep and the dog, isn't that a devil of a dog!'

'Try to keep quiet so I can get close to him!'

'Heaven help me, isn't that a devil of a dog! Look how he's catching hold of the sheep!'

I went to restrain the dog. I was kept at it like this, and William never looked like going to sleep; but finally they had to go to get the doctor. They didn't want it to become known at all, thinking that he would get better without a doctor or anything else. He would never have got better without the doctor. The doctor came, then he sent him medicine first, and said he would come back at ten o'clock on the next day. The doctor lived on the other side of the loch. When William had taken the medicine, he fell asleep, and when the doctor came the next day he was still asleep. The doctor tried his pulse, and said he was to be left undisturbed, and not to be wakened until he woke up himself. 'Don't worry about him so far as food is concerned. Leave him undisturbed though he sleeps for three days, don't waken him at all.'

That was the night I got clear of dear old William, and got to my bed, and I didn't go to a meal when I got the chance, I went straight to bed; the barmaid came to me with food, and I never saw a bit of what I ate, my two eyes were closed like an otter's, and she was beside herself laughing and making fun of me!

When I woke up, it was the evening of the next day, before I awoke, and William was still asleep then, and he spent two days and a night asleep before he awoke; and when he awoke, he was so weak he could not turn over in bed by himself. It was not that that surprised me most, but that he remembered everything he had seen much better than I did! He saw them as clearly as could be. There you have the story of William and the apparitions; indeed there was plenty to trouble him while he was seeing them!

William and the Turnips

Mr Kane and I got on very well, very little was coming between us. But I don't think anyone could have been found who was better at doing harm to himself than his son William; and so he did. He would sooner have seen his father's property on fire than have lifted a hand to put it in order. There was nothing I could do; the son didn't care if his father was consumed and ruined. It would have been better for Kane not to have had William in Ross at all.

Kane kept cattle there, and William and his wife were supposed to feed them and look after them. William was only getting a wage, like I was, he was not in charge of anything, he wasn't worthy of any charge being given to him.

I had to go down once a week to look at the place, and if there was anything wrong there, I was to tell Mr Kane himself. I never went down there that I didn't see something wrong, but if I did, I wasn't telling Kane about it; it was better for me to keep quiet.

This time, when I went down there, I went into the byre. There was no telling how long it was since a beast had been in it; it had got into a mess. I didn't know what I should do. I went and got a broom and cleaned the byre, and I cleared the courtyard. Then I took a look at the turnip shed; there was nothing in it but husks and cowdung. I cleaned the turnip shed, and then I had a look at the stack-yard. I found that the gate had been opened and the cattle let into the hayrick. I didn't know what to say. I went over to the farmhouse; only William's wife was in, William was up at the hotel. I asked her why the place was like that, how had it got into such a mess.

'Oh, I don't know,' she said. 'I was ill for the last three days, I couldn't look after anything, that's why things are the way they are.'

But I found out all right that illness had nothing to do with it, that she had been calling at the forester's house the day before! I came home. Kane asked me how things were down there? 'Oh,' I said, 'as usual.' That was all right, the matter was over. But a week later, on a Sunday, I went down to see how things were. If they had been bad before, they were ten times worse that day! I came back, without going near them. I said to myself that it was useless for me to go down, and that Kane himself must go down and look after it. That was the first thing I meant to say to him when he next asked me when I had been there.

Anyway, time went past, and nothing was said. But a week later, William came up on a cold frosty morning, and told me that I would have to go down to Ross today, that the cattle had broken into the turnip clamps in the field, and that I would have to put things right. 'Oh, indeed,' I said, 'there was nothing else you could spoil but the clamps in the field, now you've messed up the steading. Go and tell him yourself, and if he tells me to go down, I'll go down. It's useless for me to go down, I've been down often enough and I'm none the better for it.'

'Oh, I'm sure,' said William, 'it isn't my fault.'

'Oh, no, it's my fault, I'm sure,' I said.

'I didn't say that.'

'You were just next door to it,' I said. 'Go and tell it to your father.'

'I won't. I've got nothing to do with it, you're the one in charge of the place, and if you won't come, stay away, it's no business of mine.'

William went off and left me. Rob Baird, who was working along with me, asked:

'Are you going down there?'

'No,' I said. 'Are you? What's the good of my going there, when it will be in a mess before I get back?'

I went off to plough. Around eleven o'clock, I saw William's wife coming up. She went into the hotel. When I was un-hitching to come home for dinner, she was going back down the road. I could see she had left the pot on the boil!

When I came in for my dinner, Kane was laying off down in the bar, and the house was resounding to him! I went into the kitchen. In a moment I heard him coming up the passage. He called to me and asked if I was in there. I answered and said I was.

'I want to see you when you've had your dinner,' he said.

'All right.'

'Oh, hell!' he said, going back down the passage.

I was studying what I was going to say when I went to see him, I would say that it was useless for me to be going down to Ross, that he himself must go down there now, and keep an eye on it. I got up when I had finished, and went along. Kane was sitting inside the bar. He got up and came over.

'When were you down at Ross?' he asked.

'A week ago,' I said.

'How were things there then?'

'Very middling.'

'Didn't I tell you to put a fence around the turnip clamps in the corner of the field?' he said.

'You did.'

'Didn't I give you all the materials you wanted to put up a fence there?'

'You did.'

'Did you put it up?'

'Yes.'

'It was a damned poor fence,' he said, 'when my cattle broke in last night and spoilt it for me. What's the good of my keeping a man and paying him a big wage to look after my business when he doesn't give a be-damn about it? Doing what you like, taking advantage of me since I can't look after it myself?'

When I heard him start like this, I didn't say a word, but bent my head and let him speak. But it was then that he went right off the deep end. The barmaid was standing behind, nearly in tears watching me not saying a word. Kane turned and said:

'It would be better for you to steal the money out of my pocket, than to be taking wages for something you aren't doing, or looking after at all, that you don't give a be-damn about.'

'Oh, well,' I said, 'since I don't give a be-damn about your place, it's high time you got someone else who'll look after it better than I do.'

'It's high time I did,' he said.

'I believe it is. But how the devil do you think that the turnips in the field will be saved when the turnips in the shed aren't? But since you aren't able to walk down there, I'll drive you down, and you must go down there and see to it. I'm not going to be running back and forth between you and your son any longer.'

'What the devil are you saying?'

'That's what I'm saying.'

'Go and harness the black pony to the phaeton,' said Kane, 'and come here to the door.'

'Oh, it's high time you did,' I said. I went and harnessed the pony, and brought her to the door for him. Kane came out and got into the phaeton. He was terribly bad with rheumatism, in his legs, he could hardly walk. I went off with him, and oh! he didn't say a word all the way until I reached the gate of the field. When I reached the gate, I tied the pony to it. Kane stumbled out of the phaeton and went into the field. I followed him, and went past him. When I reached the turnip clamps, of which there were three side by side, they had been turned into a bog, the cattle had been in them all the week. As neat an opening as I ever saw had been made in the (wooden) fence, which had been broken with a hammer; they couldn't take the posts out, they were five and a half feet long, driven into the ground, and the nails in the posts were four inches long.

Kane came and looked and didn't say a word.

'Well,' I said, 'that's the fence I put around the turnips, what better fence than that did you want me to put there?'

'You couldn't have,' he said. 'I didn't think that this was the way of it at all.'

'I'm sure you didn't,' I said. 'It's likely I shut the cattle in along with the turnips! This fence has been broken from the inside, not from the outside. Did cattle do that?'

'No,' Kane said, 'but the devil's own two hands!'

'He wouldn't do that,' I said.

'Yes, he would, his servant would, he was always doing his service, he and the woman he got!' He broke into a sob. 'How I'm treated today by my only son!'

'Oh, well,' I said, 'that's all there is here. We'll go down and see what the rest looks like.'

We went along to the courtyard. I went into the byre, and opened the door, and oh! a stream of cow dung came out of the door. I didn't know when a beast had been inside it.

'There's a byre kept clean and tidy for you!' I said.

'Oh, well, well, well!'

I went and opened the turnip shed. 'Oh, heavens!' he said, 'that beats everything!' I went over to the stack-yard gate. The gate had been opened after I had tied it with barbed wire, back and forth, I had nearly put a roll in it! They had taken the wire away and let the cattle into the hayrick.

'Why the devil didn't you tell me about this long ago?' Kane said, 'before you let me be destroyed, that's what you've done!'

'What good would it have done to have told you? You wouldn't have believed me then, and you wouldn't have believed me today, I couldn't get to speak to you at all. When I've come down here and had to strip and start cleaning the cow-byre and the courtyard here so that it would look as if the place was inhabited, you would be asking me if I was asleep down at Ross!'

'Oh, well,' he said, 'if I happened to say that, I wasn't meaning anything by it.'

'What's been said can't be unsaid,' I replied. 'But that's all I'll do for you. Now you can get someone else to do it.'

'Oh, well, if you leave like that, you won't get a penny of your wages!'

'I'm only asking for what I've earned,' I said.

'I'm not sending you away.'

'You said I had been here too long.'

'How could I know? But why did you let me call you everything but a gentleman?'

'What could I do about it? I couldn't catch hold of your tongue!'

'Oh,' he said, 'you'll not leave like that at all.'

'Yes I will,' I said. 'Today I've stood from you what I wouldn't put up with from my own father and mother.'

Kane went off then over to the farmhouse. Only his daughter-in-law was in. Very soon she came out crying with him after her. I'm sure she had got some strokes from his stick before she managed to gain the door! Off into the wood she went past the end of the house, out of my sight, with Kane after her. When I saw him chasing her at the double I couldn't help bursting into laughter in the courtyard, for at her speed she would have been in New Zealand before he had reached the hotel! Then he came back, using terrible language. He was going to shut the door with stones, and never let any of them inside again, but 'go and camp by the high road'.

Then he reached me. 'I don't know what in the world to do here, unless you have an idea.'

'I'll have no more to do with it,' I said. 'You get another man.'

'I don't care for that kind of talk,' he said.

'I do,' I said.

'Well, I'll tell you what you'll do. As you've got a horse harnessed there, don't unhitch it at all, but bring down the other fellow and Johnny MacLaren, to see if you and he can put yon right tonight, you get Johnny to clean the byre and put in the beasts, if there's anything for them, I don't know, it's likely you'll see,' he said.

'It's not two hours work here at all,' I said.

'I know it isn't, there's two days work here, but you'll likely see tomorrow what's the best thing to do. Send Johnny down in the morning and evening to feed the cattle and let them out, those two'll do no more for me, but let them clear off to hell out of my sight. I'd never have let them in here but for his mother, spoiling him, but everyone can see it now, and could long ago. No wonder no farm-servant would stay with me.'

'The devil himself wouldn't stay with you,' I said, turning to him.

'And you run down at night and see they're being looked after.'

'I can't be coming here every evening,' I said. 'I've enough to do.'

'God bless me, I'm not meaning you to walk here, you've got plenty of ponies, you can saddle one of them, and you won't be long running back and forth.'

I said to myself that I would try it, to see if I could last the term out, anyway; it was just about half-term, the beginning of spring. Anyway, I sent Johnny down, and I and the other fellow went down the next day and took a cart with us; we mended the fence, and took what turnips were more or less whole to a river there and washed them, and put them into the stack-yard. When I went down in the evening, William's wife came out to meet me, crying. 'You needn't be sending Johnny down, we'll do it.'

'Why didn't you do it before?' I said. 'Is it my fault? It would have been all right if you could have got me blamed for it.'

'We were never blaming you, we wouldn't listen to anyone else blaming you,' she said.

I went off and left her there. When the old lady at the hotel got ahold of me she implored me to show favour to William, her only child, he'd nothing but a bad wife who wouldn't do a turn, and William was only to be pitied.

'Oh, I can't do anything,' I said, 'I can only do what Mr Kane tells me to.'

But matters came to this: before Johnny arrived to feed the cattle in the morning, William and his wife had fed them, and the byre had been cleaned; before Johnny arrived in the afternoon, the cattle had been put in. Johnny was only standing there idle. I had to send Rob Baird to feed the cattle that were up at the hotel, the stirks, morning and evening, and I had no one to help me in the stable. The day would never come that I'd ask Kane to get another man, for fear of causing another row before the term came.

William and the Deer

The matter blew over, I didn't hear anything more about it, it was all right. But there were two acres in a field above the steading at Ross which I had ploughed and sown with oats. The oats grew extremely well there. Everyone who saw them was praising them and saying how good they were, that there wasn't a bit like it in the district. They were saying this to the old man, and oh! he was going to plough a good bit next year, it would pay him better than grass there.

But one morning William came down and went to where I was in the stable.

'The deer have made a bad mess of your oats at Ross, Angus,' he said.

'Have they?'

'Oh yes, indeed.'

'You've got a good gun, haven't you? Why don't you take it with you and shoot them?'

'Oh, I can't do that.'

'Who's stopping you?'

'Who isn't? You should speak to the gamekeeper.'

I saw the gamekeeper, then, down on the pier and went over to him.

'I hear your deer have made a bad mess of the oats at Ross, that you aren't keeping an eye on them at all,' I said.

'Did you see them there yourself?'

'No, indeed; they could be there often enough without my seeing them.'

'Oh, I don't believe the deer are going there.'

'Well, if you don't, if I see one there, it'll stay there, I'll shoot it; you'll believe me then.'

'Don't spare it,' he said.

My word, it surprised me that he would give me leave to kill the deer. I couldn't say anything. That night, the old man sent the barmaid to fetch me; I went in.

'When were you at Ross?' he said.

'I was down there at the end of last week.'

'Were you at the oats?'

'No.'

'William is telling me that the deer have spoilt them.'

'Yes, I heard him say that.'

'Have you seen the gamekeeper?'

'I have.'

'What did he say?'

'He didn't believe they were going there at all.'

'What did you say to him?'

'I said that if I saw a deer there, it would stay there, I would shoot it.'

'You said the right thing to him. But you should go down with the gun, and if you see the deer there, just put a bullet in it.'

'Can't William take the gun?' I said. 'He could put a bullet in them, and stop them going there.'

'William! William couldn't hit Ben Lomond! You'd better go down.'

Well, I had plenty to do where I was, but the next day it was wet, and I wasn't doing much. I went in for my tea at four o'clock, and Kane came along.

'When you've had your tea, Angus, take the gun and go down to Ross, and if there's a deer there just shoot it and leave it there.'

I went off when I had had my tea, taking the gun and two cartridges of swan-shot. There was a short cut through the wood, only half as far (as the road). When I reached the field, my word, there was a deer in the oats, up beyond the gate. There was a stone wall on one side of the oats, and a fence on the other. The deer was on the side near the stone wall.

I began to creep round until I got to the wall. I went on my knees up along the wall. When I thought I was more or less even with the place where I had seen the deer, I looked between the stones. The deer was just in front of me and only ten yards away. Its back was turned to me. When it raised its head, I could see the tip of its antlers; when it lowered its head, I could only see its back. It was no use firing at it until it turned side on to me.

The deer didn't turn, it kept going away from me. I was afraid it would go too far from me and that I would lose it altogether. I said to myself I would raise the gun to the top of the wall, and when the deer lifted its head, I would give it the first cartridge in the back of its head, and the second would be in its heart before it went over the wall. I cocked both hammers and—then yon thing swept round its head with a wisp of oats in its mouth, and woe is me, what had I got but William's red cow! I nearly fell in a faint, for if I had killed it, I would never have got over the disgrace, killing a cow by mistake for a deer! All I did was to get behind her and go down to the steading with her. She was bulging, hardly able to walk with what she had inside her; she had been let into the field every day! That was why the gamekeeper had given me leave to kill the deer, he knew what it was all right, but he wouldn't tell me.

I went into the house. William's wife was inside. 'Come out, now, you devil,' I said, 'and see the deer that's been spoiling the oats. Your own cow in them every day!'

'Oh, she was never there, unless she got in today!'

'Hasn't she been in there every day? Wasn't that why MacGregor was giving me leave to kill the deer if I saw it there? But I'll be telling the boss, and he'll read you the riot act!'

Oh, then she began to make up to me. 'She'll never go there again, someone must have left the gate open.'

I said to myself that it was no use for me to go and tell Kane, the oats were spoilt anyway, and it was just as well to let things be. But I was feeling it long enough until the term came, and I made up my mind that when the term came, I wouldn't stay there, that it would take rifle and bayonet to make me stay there another six months between Kane and his son!

How I Left Old Kane

I had made up my mind I was going to leave this year, at Whitsuntide, six months before I left. Kane asked what was making me leave.

'I must go home,' I said, 'my father and mother are alone at home, and they're getting old.'

'Well,' he said, 'I think it would be better for you to get a lad or a girl to stay with your mother and father, and to keep on at your job, it would pay you better. Though you paid them yourself, I'm sure they wouldn't cost you much.'

'Oh, my wages aren't that big I can afford to pay a servant at all.'

'Well, that's what you'd best do,' he said, 'and I'll give you a rise of a pound.'[39]

Well, this was very good; when I heard it, I agreed to stay until Martinmas, and I engaged with Kane for another six months. But then, when I saw how things were going, I swore that I would sooner be shot and bayoneted than spend a further six months working for him! Anyway, when it was drawing near to the Martinmas term, I got the harvest in pretty early and got in the oats and the hay in beautiful weather.

Then there came a fortnight of dry weather with an easterly wind. There was a lot of bracken down at a place called Millarachy three miles south of the hotel. I thought that it would be a good thing if some of the bracken was cut and brought home for bedding. I went with another fellow and we spent all day scything bracken there. When we had come home that night, Kane sent for me to come to the bar, and I went.

'Where were you today?' he asked.

'Down at Millarachy cutting bracken,' I said.

'Is there good bracken there?' he said.

'Oh yes, indeed,' I said.

'Well, you'll be lucky if you got it home in this dry spell.'

'My word, it's ripe anyway, if I get just one dry day I can get it put up in the stack.'

We then began to take it home. We were taking out two loads a day. Well, we put a dozen cartloads in the stack, and then I cut a cartload of rushes to thatch it. This afternoon when it had been put up for a week, I was going to thatch it. I asked Baird to go and clean the saddles down below, and oil them and put them away. I went to thatch the stack. Whom did I see limping over but the old man himself, with his stick; he was fearfully bad with rheumatism.

'Well, indeed,' he said, 'I don't think you'll have to buy straw this year.'

'Well, I don't think you'll need to buy so much, when there's bedding down at Millarachy,' I said.

'Oh, yes,' he said, 'but who would take the trouble to fetch it? Wouldn't a bale of straw be handy?'

'Yes,' I said, 'but you don't get straw for nothing.'

'No, you don't.'

Then he began to tell me what he was spending on bedding every year, and that wasn't a little. The horses were indoors summer and winter.

'Well, I think this is just as good as straw for bedding,' I said.

'It's much better,' he said, 'and it's good for the land too. Are you on your own?'

'Yes.'

'Where's Rob?'

'I told him to clean the saddles and put them away, they won't be needed again this year.'

'You can't do without someone here,' he said.

'Oh, he'll come over to help me put the ropes on the stacks, when I'm ready.'

'All right,' said Kane. 'Well, then, I came over to see you, I wanted to tell you the idea I had. I'm thinking of keeping Johnny MacLaren (the lad who was looking after the cattle) along with you this winter, he'd give you a hand, he'd do the ferry for you.' (I had to attend to the ferry too.)

'Oh, Johnny's a handy lad right enough,' I said.

'And I was thinking I wouldn't get a boots before July,' Kane said, 'and that you could take the boots' place until then, after Johnny comes to help you; but what I wanted to tell you was that I can only give you fourteen pounds in the half-year; but your wages for the six months after will be as high as they are now.'

Well, when I heard this! This was going to take two pounds off my wages[40] and give me more to do!

'Oh, well,' I said, 'I think that it's enough for me to be looking for another place.'

'What's that you say?'

'When you're lowering my wages.'

'I'm raising your wages, see what a chance you'll get.'[41]

'Oh well, if that's the way I'm getting a chance, it wouldn't put a penny in my pocket, and I'd have to work for it, many a night I'd have to be at work cleaning shoes and spoons until midnight, when I should be in bed, and my work to do over and above.'

'Well,' he said, 'I could get plenty who'd take your place for less than that.'

'All right,' I said, 'don't put yourself to any loss on my account. I can just as easily get a master as you can get a servant.'

'Oh, well,' said Kane, 'if that's the way you take it, try and better yourself, then.'

'Oh, that's what everyone tries to do, anyway.'

Kane went off kicking pebbles before him; his plan hadn't worked at all! He went into the harness-room where Rob Baird was cleaning the saddles. This is what he told him:

'I was over in the stack-yard speaking to that Angus to stay here for the winter. I was going to keep Johnny MacLaren along with him and give him fourteen pounds wages and the boots' place until July, until the hay-time; and he got annoyed with me.'

'Well, I think you did very well,' said Rob.

'Yes, I think I did,' said Kane, 'but the more a man gets the more he asks for. But there's nothing for him now but to try to find another place.'

When Rob came over to rope the stacks with me, he said:

'Well, you're foolish if you don't accept it.'

'Well, I'm not going to,' I said.

'You'd better take it now you've got the chance.'

'Haven't you got the chance now, you take it,' I said.

'Oh, I'd take the boots' place, but I can't take your place. I can't plough or do anything else like that like you can.'

'Can't you learn?'

'It's too late now, but, by God, you won't let anyone else do it.'

'My word, I'll let anyone you like. You won't see me here after midday on term-day. I'm not going to be in the middle between him and his son any more.'

'Ah, well, you're not the first man that that put out of the place. This would be a good place if William were in hell, himself and his wife!'

That was that. Then we were coming near to the time of the hiring fare, it was going to be next day, as it were. Rob and I were in the stable, and I asked him:

'Are you going to the hiring fair tomorrow?'

'No,' he said, 'I've no reason for going there.'

'Why?'

'There'll only be jobs with farmers, and I can't take those. I'll go to Glasgow at the term, and maybe I'll get a job driving a van or something. Are you going to the fair yourself?'

'Yes,' I said.

'You'll easily get a place if you don't stay where you are.'

'I'm not going to stay where I am,' I said, 'he's been told that already.'

'Well, I don't believe he thinks so.'

'I don't care what he thinks.'

Anyway, next day in the morning when we were in the stable, I said to Rob:

'When you've had your breakfast, harnesss that horse and start putting out dung to the field where the turnips are going to be. Make dung-heaps inside the gate.'

'Oh yes,' he said, 'haven't you anything sooner done than that to give me, when you're going off to play yourself?'

'What work can I give you unless you go and plough?'

'I won't go,' he said. 'I can't plough.'

'Are you asking to be sitting there?' I said.

'That's not the way of it; I'm going to the hiring fair myself.'

'Oh, all right,' I said, 'if you are, I can't keep you, nor can your master, but why didn't you tell me that yesterday? I would have told himself; someone has to be here at dinner-time to give food and water to the horses.'

'Well, there isn't anything for it but for you to go and tell him today.'

I went off, and we went up to our breakfast. When we had had our breakfast, I got up and went down to the bar. Only the barmaid was there, Lizzie MacKay, a girl from Inverness.

'Off you go, dearie, upstairs where the boss is and tell him we're going to the hiring fair,' I said, 'so he can speak to William or someone to give food and water to the horses at dinner-time.'

She ran up the stairs. I waited at the foot of the staircase. My dear, I heard hallooing above, and the house resounding to it! I realized that the thorn had pricked the toad! Lizzie came down the stairs as red as a crab.

'Well, the next time you have a message to send, Angus, you'll go with it yourself!'

'What did he do to you?' I asked.

'He didn't do anything to me, he didn't dare to.'

'What did he say to you?'

'Plenty.'

'Did he say to you I wouldn't get to go?'

'Well, he said to me as I was coming out of the door, that you could go, but that you should have told him yesterday.'

'The wretch,' I said. 'It's three weeks since I told him I wasn't staying. Won't do that for him? Let him blow off there!'

We went to the hiring fair. I didn't engage at it at all. Wages were pretty low at the time, and it was mostly bothying down that way, with oatmeal and milk.[42] Anyway, we stayed at a dance in the village until after midnight, and it was one in the morning when we got home. We didn't go to bed at all, but lay for a while on our beds with our clothes on. In the morning we harnessed the horses and started to put out dung. We spent just three days putting out dung, until we had cleaned the farmyard. The last cart we took, in the twilight, I took a grape with me. I was squaring up the dung-hills, and I called to Rob to bring the two carts up with him and unharness them. When I was finished, I looked up and who was coming up to me but old Kane.

'Well, indeed,' he said, 'you did very well to put the dung

out while you've got help, before Rob leaves.' I wasn't to be leaving at all!

'Oh, I think it's better here, anyway, than inside.'

'I think it is,' he said. Then he began to talk about what he meant to do in the winter; there was a little field over beside the wood, which he called the 'Wood Field'. 'Do you think that oats would grow in the Wood Field over there, if it were ploughed?'

'I'm sure they would,' I said, 'it's early in the winter.'

'Well, I was thinking,' said Kane, 'that clover might be got to grow in it, it would be good for the calves.'

'The calves are in need of some kind of a good place,' I said.

This was all right. I was waiting for him—his stride was no longer than a hen's with his rheumatism—until we reached the gate, and then I was going to go ahead. He stopped.

'Rob tells me you didn't engage at the fair at all.'

'I didn't.'

'Well, you did the right thing, and you won't regret it; I'll be as good to you as I said.'

'Oh, I hope you haven't let slip the chance of getting another man on account of me,' I said.

'I haven't spoken to anyone,' said Kane. 'I wasn't going to speak to anyone until you had left me.'

'My word, isn't it four weeks since I told you I'm not going to stay?'

'Are you still of that mind?'

'Yes, indeed I am.'

'Well, I never saw anyone so obstinate as you are. Anything you say you won't depart from.'

'I'm not obstinate,' I said, 'nor anything of the kind. Isn't it easy enough for you to get another man for less than me? Why don't you do it?'

My word, he wouldn't listen to this at all.

'Well,' he said, 'if I was going to take two pounds off your pay, I'm sure I was going to put it back three times over; if that's what you're complaining of, it won't make me much poorer than I am, you can have the wages you're getting. Such a devil I never saw! It's simply wages for being asleep, you

147

know very well that you won't be allowed to sleep until eight o'clock everywhere.' (It was he himself who was asking us to stay in bed in winter-time and not get up before dawn, for fear of wasting light.)

Oh dear! 'Tut, tut, tut!' I said. 'Don't put yourself out for my sake! I'd not stay now although you gave me fifty pounds in the half year!'

'If you won't,' he said, 'you can go to hell!'

'Oh, many thanks, I'll leave that place to you along with Rowardennan!'

Kane went in. He was holding forth in the bar. When we went in for our supper, the cook asked me:

'Upon my soul, what have you done to the boss?'

'We haven't done anything to him, we didn't say a word to him.'

'Maybe not, but he's wild with anger.'

'Tut, that's not a serious complaint,' I said.

Never mind, next day we went to the stable. It was a pretty cold day too. There was no more room between the bothy in which we slept and the door of the kitchen than would let a cart pass. There were three or four good-sized stones lying beside the bothy door, and their marks were on it.

'My word,' I said, 'see the stones that were thrown at the door. Who did that?'

'That damned fellow,' said Rob, 'Johnny MacIntyre (the son of the forester down the loch) was up seeing Mary Campbell last night, he thought we hadn't got up, he wanted to take a rise out of us.'

'I didn't see anyone on the road,' I said.

'He would take care you didn't see him on the road, he would go through the wood.'

That was that. Next morning, when we came down, the stones were there again.

'Look, they're at the door again today,' I said.

'Oh,' said Rob, 'that fellow doesn't sleep a night at home. Don't let on. We'll watch him after this.'

All right. The next day was very cold with a north-east wind and snow showers. I got up before five o'clock. We didn't get our breakfast before eight. We were in the stable; we had finished with the horses, and were watching the kitchen chimney to see if we could see smoke coming from it. There was none to be seen. Rob turned to me and said:

'You dirty dog, getting men out of bed at five in the morning! You should be in bed yet, you won't get your breakfast until eight o'clock.'

'I don't care if he wouldn't give us breakfast until it was ten o'clock; that's all we'll do until we do get our breakfast.'

'Didn't he tell you many a time that you didn't need to get up until it was near daytime?'

'Oh, we heard him saying something else then,' I said.

'I don't care about that,' Rob said.

'Oh no, but I do.'

'Well, indeed, I think it's time to be leaving here right enough. If you were another year here along with us all that would be left of us would be our shoes.'

'Oh, well then, you'll get plenty of sleep, I won't be here much longer. But come along here, we'll get better shelter than this.'

There was a garden between the stable and the bothy. We went through. The harness-room was just at the end of the bothy. 'Come in here,' I said, 'until they get up. This is much warmer.'

We went in, and Rob pushed the door to. But then we heard one of the hotel windows being opened. Rob looked out through the crack of the door. Who was it there but the boss!

'Oh, the boss!' said Rob, 'he's looking out to see what's the day like!'

'What's up with him today, do you know?' I said.

'I don't know.'

But it wasn't long before there came a stone which made a noise against the door of the bothy. Rob looked at me and his colour changed.

'Yon devil,' he said, 'he's the one who was throwing the stones!'

'Yes,' I said. 'Don't you be telling me off now for waking you at five o'clock. Now do you see who it is?'

Another stone came, and a third, striking the bothy door so

neatly. I was waiting to see if Kane would come out and open the door. But then he lent out of the window and shouted:

'Get up out of there, you lazy b——rs! There's my lads for you, wanting big pay for being asleep!'

Rob turned to me: 'Get out and speak to him, it's your place.'

I jumped out of the door.

'Hullo, Mr Kane!' I said. 'You're throwing those stones the wrong way. You should have thrown them at your women-folk down there so they'll give us our breakfast, if you're in such a hurry. We didn't know who was throwing those stones at the bothy door until now, but the next time I catch you throwing them I'll knock you down with one of them!'

Down came the window! It wasn't long before we saw smoke coming from the kitchen chimney. We went in. 'Sit down there now,' I said, 'until we get our breakfast.'

'What on earth's wrong with Mr Kane?' said the maid.

'I don't know what's wrong with him.'

Then the mistress came down herself. How she was scolding! 'The miserable wretch! The wicked fellow! Don't pay heed to him! Why are you getting up before daylight? Wasting light!'

All Kane could do was to turn and go away, I'd say as if to please himself. But the stones stopped!

The last week felt long enough. And the worst of it was that term-day, the twenty-eighth (of November), was falling on a Sunday.[43] We should be getting away on the Saturday, we expected to. But did we?

I began to collect all my belongings on Saturday morning. I had everything together by dinner-time. The carts had been washed and put into the sheds. Kane should have come out then and seen them, but he didn't come outside. After we had had our dinner, I got up and went down to the bar. The bar-maid was the only person I found there.

'Where's Mr Kane?' I said.

'He's in bed.'

'Damn it, doesn't he mean to let us away today?'

'I believe that's the last thought in his head.'[44]

'He won't be much the better for keeping us here until Monday.'

'Oh, won't he satisfy his own nature?' she said.

'If he'll do that, that's the way he'll be.'

I went back to the kitchen. Rob asked:

'Did you get clear?'

'No,' I said.

'Did you see him?'

'No, he's in bed.'

'Well, you can go up and make him let us away.'

'Indeed I won't,' I said. 'But though he's kept us tonight, he won't keep us on Monday.'

We got up and went out.

'What are you going to do now?' Rob asked.

'Very little. We'll go down and bale the boats if there's any water in them. I'll do no more than that. I won't take out a horse again.'

'That's all right, I don't mind,' said Rob.

All the other farmers' men got away that night. They collected down at the hotel, a tremendous crowd. There were some men working at woodcutting up the loch; they came too. I saw it was going to be a rough night, and I said to Rob:

'If there's anything in the bothy that you need before you go to bed, take it with you, and we'll stay in the kitchen until they go away. If we come out of here we'll never get clear of them tonight.'

'Oh, there's nothing I need, you can lock the bothy up.'

I went and locked the door. We went into the kitchen. When we had had our supper, we played draughts and cards there. Drinking was going on down in the tap-rooms. The girl was serving them. When it was ten o'clock, and they were put out, they stayed around the hotel, and weren't going away. We stayed in the kitchen until they cleared off; we knew that if we went out they would come into the bothy along with us.

It was getting on for eleven o'clock. Everyone had gone to bed except the kitchenmaids. We didn't hear anything outside; we went out. They had cleared off. We went into the bothy and lit a candle. We were going to bed, I had just shut

the bothy door—it was freezing, a dead calm frosty night—
when I heard a g-r-o-a-n over near the tap-room, and the
ugliest sound of grinding teeth I ever heard.

'My goodness,' I said, 'what's that?'

'I don't know,' said Rob.

'Go and look,' I said.

Rob went. 'By God, there's a man here!'

'Who is it?' I said.

'I don't know. Bring a light.'

Rob started to speak to him; the man paid no heed. 'The
fellow's done for,' said Rob.

I lit the lantern, and went over. Well, we recognized him at
once, he was an Irish lad who was working in the woods.
He surely had been poisoned! He couldn't speak a word, but
how he was shivering! I looked; there was no one in the
kitchen, no light or anything else there.

'Upon my soul,' I said, 'what will we do with him?'

'We'll carry him into the bothy,' said Rob.

We lifted him into the bothy between us, and we put him
to lie on sacks on the floor, and put horse rugs over him. He
had a flask in his pocket; we took the flask from him and put
it on the window-sill, and 'if you live, you'll need it, and if
you don't, they'll likely open it at your funeral'. We didn't
dare to go to bed in case he'd be dead before we woke up.
All we did was watch him there. When it was getting on
towards daytime, he was getting warm under the rugs, and I
said that we must try to get him away. We lifted him up and
put him sitting in a chair. Well, he could speak then. We
gave him the flask, and he took a drop or two out of it. He
was getting better.

'Come on now,' I said, 'see if you can get home.'

We went off with him. He was getting better all the time.
When we were up near the hut, he said:

'By the Book, I'll manage the rest by myself.'

Then he wanted to insist on us taking a share of the contents of his flask, but we wouldn't take a drop, 'Keep it yourself, it'll do for your "morning!"' We went back. There wasn't
time to go to bed, but we lay for a while on top of the bed in
our clothes, and then we went to the stable. We used to get

breakfast at nine o'clock on Sundays. When we had had our breakfast, we went out to the bothy, and began to wash ourselves and to put on clean clothes, we weren't putting on working clothes again. I was busy packing my chest, and Rob himself was opposite me packing. Who came out but the boss with his stick. He came over and stood in the door of the bothy.

'Well, indeed,' he said, 'I think it's high time for you to be packing up, if that's the work you've been at since last night came, drinking and blackguarding from then till now, drinking with every blackguard in the country!' Wasn't that hard? Rob looked at me. I hung my head and kept my mouth shut, and said nothing. It wasn't what he had said that had hurt me, but how pleased he was to have something on us, it seemed. When he was just turning to go out of the door, I turned and said to him:

'Well, thank you for our characters on the last day.'

'You're welcome,' he said.

'So I understand,' I said. 'That's all the thanks we get today for screening you since last night came.'

'I'm not obliged to anyone for screening me.'

'If you weren't, we would have left the man at your tap-room door, and he'd be dead today, the man you left last night dead with poison, that's what you gave him, not drink; you'd know differently!'

By God, he grew as pale as a sheet.

'If you're trying to spoil my character, you won't succeed, I'm too knowledgeable; my work can be seen and I'm not ashamed of it; but I hope that you'll get someone who'll keep what you need on your place.'

'You wouldn't keep me in it,' he said.

'I didn't try to,' I said. 'If I had, I would have kept you there, and I'm very sorry I didn't do it; and if you speak another two words, I'll let it be known and likely make you lose your licence, long as you've been mixing poison here and selling it for whisky to the public.' I was telling the truth. 'And sending us out to poach at night during close-time as well!'

How he doubled in through the door! 'It's just as well for ye,' I said, 'to clear out of my sight!'

Rob went off to the stable. We fed the horses, and he asked me:

'Are you going to stay here?'

'Where else would you stay, until you got your wages?'

'You're damned low if you're going to stay here after what's been said to you, that it was high time you left.'

'Are you going to stay yourself?' I said.

'No, I won't eat another bite inside his house as long as I live.'

'Where are you going?'

'I'd sooner go where you do.'

'You're welcome.'

'We'll go up to the gamekeeper's house.'

'Come along then,' I said.

We went along. Dinner was ready on the table (in the hotel kitchen), and when they saw us going off, they had no doubt whatever that we were going to report them! Kane's wife and son started on him, crying out like stuck pigs, so the servant said. We didn't come back. We wouldn't get the steamer until nine o'clock the next morning. We came back at eight o'clock, and went straight to the bothy and lifted out our chests. William was along with Kane in the bar; Kane sent him out, and he asked us to come in. We went in. He had my wages counted out on the counter. He pointed to them.

'Count that,' he said.

I counted it.

'Is that right?'

'Yes.'

'Well,' he said, 'and I gave you a week's holiday last year, and you took a fortnight, and I had to give another man a pound until you came back.'

'Why didn't you keep it off?' I said.

'Well, I didn't, but I could have kept it.'

'I'd sooner you had,' I said. 'How many times have I worked for you until midnight or one in the morning without charging you for it? See you don't deal with the next farm-servant you get as you've dealt with me on the last day.'

I simply turned out of the door. His poor wife—the old

lady was awfully nice—was standing in the passage, and 'good-bye, Angus' she said 'may the day never come that you're better off than I could wish; what peace has ever been here, has been since you came'.

That's how I left the lame old fellow on the last day!

6

DALMALLY

WHEN I first went to Dalmally, to the hotel, I left home a little after New Year, I had come home for the winter to be along with my father and mother after I left Rowardennan. There was no employment at home that would keep me, and I went to Oban and got work on the railway pier, which was being made bigger. I saw this situation advertised in the paper, wanting a ploughman for Dalmally Hotel, and I put in for it, and got it. I went on to Dalmally. There were plenty of men there, but there was only one I knew, a fellow from Perthshire called Alec Robertson, whom I had known well when I was in Perthshire, at Aberfeldy.

The two of us were working together every day. I arrived on a Monday; the next Friday Robertson went with a hire to Loch Awe, and I went to lift potatoes.[1] When he was going off, he said to me:

'See and unhitch, Angus, a little before time; they'll want you all to be at dinner together, to save the hall-maid trouble.'

The field was some distance from the house, and when it was getting near to time, I thought I could do another round before time was up, but it was just twelve o'clock before I got back. All I did was to unhitch the horses and jump on to one of them; when I reached the farmyard, they were in at their dinner. I put the horses into the stable, and went in. Well, when he went in, Robertson had asked the hall-maid, 'Has Angus come yet?'

'No, he's not come yet.'

Well, there was soup and meat for dinner.

'Well,' said Robertson, 'you'd better look for his dinner.'

'Isn't his dinner there?' she said.

'He won't take that today,' he said.

'Oh, Angus isn't a Catholic.'

'Aye? You know best. Off you go,' said Robertson, 'and tell herself, or tell the cook.'

'No, I won't.'

'Well, it's better for you to go there than for me.'

'You go yourself,' she said, 'since you like him so much.'

'You liked him well enough before,' he said, 'and you may yet; but if he doesn't get better than Calum, he won't stay here, and it'll be a pity.' Calum was a lad from Taynuillt; his people had come from Canna. Nicolson was his surname.

Alec Robertson got up and went along to the mistress of the house, who was in the bar.

'What's wrong, Alec?' she asked.

'Oh, nothing, but yon new man who came today won't eat soup or meat today.'

'It would be a poor thing for us,' she said, 'if we haven't something he'll take.'

'He hasn't come in yet,' said Alec, 'but, indeed, he isn't hard to satisfy.'

'Tell him his dinner will be along presently.'

'There's a lad in the hall there,' said Alec, 'for weeks, and he has nothing better than dry bread today.'

'Who?' she said.

'Calum Nicolson.'

Right away she called the hall-maid. She asked her what was the reason she hadn't told her that there were men in the hall who didn't take soup or meat today.

'What chance did I have to do that?' said the hall-maid.

'You had the chance to, you wretch,' said the mistress. 'But for a little I'd give you the door.'

A little later, she came along, and when I went in, there was a plateful of soup at my place. Alec took away the plate of soup, and put it on the window-sill. 'Sit down,' he said, 'your dinner will be along presently.'

'It's soon enough,' I said.

She came along then with two trout, two good-sized ones

too. I looked up and saw Calum at the other end of the table, with a tumbler of milk and some bread.

'Send your plate along, Calum,' I said. 'They must have given you Friday today too.' I divided one of the trout into two halves and gave one-half to Calum and took the other half myself, and I divided the other trout amongst the rest. No doubt I was all right ever after, there wasn't one Friday as long as I was there that fish didn't come over from Inveraray on Thursday, and anyone who wouldn't take soup or meat, would get fish.

Indeed, I was very happy there, and as for kindness, the mistress used to tell the servants to see that the young fellows working there didn't go hungry, that they needed food often. We used to get our breakfast at seven o'clock in the morning; and if we were near the house, we would get tea at ten. We used to get dinner at twelve, and tea at four o'clock in the afternoon, and supper at seven; and before we went to bed at ten, we used to get tea or coffee or cocoa or whatever we preferred to take. It was as good a house for food as I was ever at.

The Ploughing Match

There was a ploughing-match at Dalmally on the farm of Fraser the hotelkeeper; and this fellow Alec Robertson, who came from a place near Aberfeldy called Tom a' Phuill, in Perthshire, that was the name of his father's farm, was an extremely good ploughman. He had got a plough made for himself, and for his brother; this plough was doing nothing all the year long, it was only for the ploughing-match. He sent to his brother in Perthshire to ask for the plough, and his brother sent it to him. There were wheels on it.

The day they were going to plough the field, there wasn't a man in Dalmally who had ever used a plough with wheels. They could have anyone along with them; and I went along with Alec. When they started, and Alec put the wheels on the plough, and opened the first furrow on top of the ridge, it was so straight that a bullet would not have knocked an eighth of an inch off it. Well, when the others saw this—they hadn't got wheels at all—they began to complain and to say that they weren't going to keep on if one man was working with wheels and the next man hadn't got wheels at all; that Alec must take the wheels off his plough.

Well, the judge was a man called McKillop, he was a ground officer. He went to see Fraser and told him he must ask his man there to take the wheels off the plough, or else no one would do a turn there today but himself; that the others had stopped, saying it wasn't right for one man to be plough-ing with wheels on his plough, and the next not having wheels at all.

'I wasn't meaning they should turn there at all,' said Fraser. 'Why didn't they reach the fence with the furrows?'

'Oh, that's not what I'm talking about at all,' said McKillop 'but that you must speak to the fellow to take the wheels off the plough.'

'I'll make them reach it yet,' said Fraser, 'it's not right to be turning there.'

'Oh, it's long since I heard "what I don't like I won't hear",[2] said McKillop. He came around quietly to where we were.

'Well, Alec,' he said, 'you're annoying plenty of people today. But will you be able to plough without wheels?'

'I will,' said Alec.

'Oh, well then,' said McKillop, 'I'm not asking you to take them off the plough, but if you can manage without them, it'll be better.'

'Oh, all right,' said Alec.

He took the wheels off the plough then; and if it wasn't much better without them, it wasn't any worse. He won all the first prizes; he cleared the field. He got the first prize for the best first furrow, and he got the first for the levellest, and he got the first for the best ploughman, and he got the first for the finish, and the first for the straightest; he won all the first prizes. Well, then they were put to shame that they didn't let him leave the wheels on the plough, they would have had some excuse!

The Mare

I saw a mare belonging to Fraser, the hotelkeeper at Dalmally, and she was as good a beast as I ever saw at work as long as she was in good humour. But maybe she'd start within five minutes. Then she'd only begin to kick the cart and squeal and bolt; then you might as well unharness her and put her indoors. Though you were to kill her, she wouldn't do anything right. When she had been inside for a day, the next day when she was taken out she would be as quiet as could be. Though I were to leave her half a mile away, she would stand there watching me until I called to her, and as soon as I called to her, she would come with the cart, and though there were a dozen gates before her, she'd go through every one of them, without grazing them; but you couldn't trust her.

They told me, and it was true, what the cause of it was; she had been running in double harness at first, she and a sister of hers, and they had been beside each other in the stable, and her sister had died in the stable and had been dragged out from the stable by a horse. Well, that day she began, and she was never again right afterwards, and they never dared to put another horse beside her in the stall after that, the stall beside her had to be empty, or else she would kick it into matchwood! Wasn't that odd? She was just nervous, she didn't know what she was doing, until she settled down.

One day I tried to work her putting in hay. I put a twitch in her nose, and a twitch in her ear, and I put a chickenstrap on her. I don't know in the world how she was bending herself but she was striking the front of the cart with her hooves, and at last I had to let her out and put her indoors; she was a white horse, but that evening she was black with sweat, streaming off her. She was always like that.

The Best Driver in Scotland

One MacColl was coming over from Inveraray, driving the four-in-hand. He had nineteen persons on board. When he was descending the hill at Cladich, the guard put on the break. The brake broke, and the guard jumped off. MacColl did not know what in the world to do; what he did was to let them have it with the whip, even if he had tried to stop, they couldn't have managed to stop the coach.

He came through the bridge at Cladich, with the wheel an inch from the parapet of the bridge, and he came safely into the station. The passengers on the coach, he had nineteen of them, make a collection of seventeen pounds for him, and his name was in the paper as the best driver in Scotland, and I'm certain they could call him that. I saw the man right enough, Duncan MacColl he was called.

The First Motor-Car I Ever Saw

I was at Dalmally when I saw the first motor-car I ever saw. That was when they first came out, and they weren't closed at all, but open on top. I didn't know what kind of thing in the world it was, when I saw it go past as I was coming home with a cartload of oats! There was neither steam nor horse nor anything in it. It went up past. There were plenty of them going on the road then when they first began. The horses were terrified of them. I think it was the smell of the oil that caused them to be. They pay no heed to them today, anyway.

The Thief

When I was at Dalmally, we had a gardener who was very bad for stealing. One of the men was going to Stirling to the Highland Society's Show. He was getting dressed and the beasts were going up to the station. He called to me as I was going to the stable, going to put the grubber through the turnips. I went up the stairs.

'There's a little something here,' he said, 'you keep it for me until I come and I'll make use of it then.'

'What is it?' I said.

'Ten pounds. It's not safe to leave it in a chest here.'

'Isn't the post office before you up there,' I said. 'Why don't you put it in there? It'll be safe enough there.'

'My word, it would be a good post office where I'd put it. Take it.'

I didn't dare not to. I would have it all night under my head, under my pillow, and all day in my pocket, until he came back at the end of the week. When he came:

'Here it is now,' I said. 'Keep it yourself now. Likely I'll get some sleep tonight.'

He began to laugh. 'Well, I wasn't afraid for it at all.'

'Oh, you weren't,' I said. 'If I had lost it, I'd only have had to leave you my wages in its place.'

'Oh, you wouldn't have needed to,' he said. 'If you had lost it, you wouldn't have lost it willingly. It isn't safe to leave anything here. Look at yon rascal, that dirty gardener, the night Johnny Miller came over from Inveraray, he was wet; he took off his trousers, and he had twenty-five shillings in his pocket; he only put his trousers on a chair by the fire, and went in to his supper. While he was having his supper, the gardener went up before him. Johnny was climbing the stairs, he heard himself the clink of money while he was climbing them; when he got up, there wasn't a penny in the pocket, it had been taken by that fellow.'

Wasn't he a tinker? He was like that, it was no good for you to risk anything at all, but indeed, the other men, they were good fellows, every one of them.

Anderson

One Saturday night the gardener and another fellow, Donald Anderson, a stonemason who lived on the other side of the river across from the hotel, were in the hotel drinking all evening. This Anderson was a terrible fellow for fighting and quarrelling; he was never anywhere but he had a row there. Anderson got a bottle of whisky to take home at ten o'clock. The gardener got a chance and stole the bottle from him, and ran upstairs with it, and put it in his chest, and threw off his clothes, and got into bed.

Well, nobody was allowed into the two rooms where we used to sleep—they were inside the hotel, but the door by which we came in was on the ground level outside. We didn't dare let in anyone after ten o'clock. The other people were sleeping in the room that was just beside us. The gardener knew this all right. He went to bed; no one would come in any more.

I had gone to bed, and the lad who was driving the (horse) bus between the hotel and the station was getting undressed to go to bed. He was a young fellow, too, who belonged to Taynuilt. But then we heard damning and cursing coming up the stairs, and who was it but Anderson the stonemason! The other lad jumped down to the door and closed it, so that Anderson wouldn't be let in, and he himself stood at the door.

Anderson began to beat on the door. The other fellow told him to clear off, that nobody was to get in here any more. The gardener was pretending to be asleep, the dirty thief! Anderson had to get in.

'You won't get in!'

'If I don't, I'll smash the door!'

Then he began kicking the door. The other fellow turned to me. I was in bed.

'My God, Angus, you must get up. He'll break down the door.'

I got up. I didn't dress at all, I only went to the door in my shirt. I shouted to him in English to clear off or else he'd get a bucket of water about his head. 'Tell him to clear away. Clear away out of here!'[3]

'Do you speak Gaelic?'

'No, I've no Gaelic!'[4]

'You've no Gaelic, you b——! You devil's brat! You so and so! You keep quiet.' Then he turned to English. 'Open the door, please.'[4]

'No.'

Then he turned nasty. He wouldn't clear off unless I knocked him down the stairs. He began to abuse me in Gaelic. The other fellow was going crazy with laughter behind me, thinking I wasn't understanding him at all. Then he began kicking the door. Then I went and turned the bolt and opened the door like this, and put my shoulder to it, to see if I could bring him to his senses.

'Ah, well,' I said, 'I'd think that you'd be ashamed at making this kind of row at such a time of night. A man with a wife and grown-up family! Why don't you come tomorrow and see the gardener, if you've got something to see him about? Don't you know very well that we aren't allowed to let anyone in here after ten o'clock!'

He lifted his arm. 'Do you see that?' he said, raising his fist. 'There's not in Glenorchy will put it back.'

'Oh, that's all right,' I said, 'but you take my advice and away home like a man.'⁵

He just went and swung his fist then to give it me right in the mouth! I ducked, and it was the door that got the blow. Well, the devil! I lost my temper at his meanness in trying to strike me when I wasn't dressed. I pulled back the door and hit him right in his stomach. He went backwards and struck the stair-rails and went down on to the road! I had no doubt at all that he had broken his neck, and I'd sooner my arm was broken in two! I went out to the stairs. I was going to report it at once. But then I heard him getting up on his knees down on the road. He was saying:

'You've done it! You devil's own b——, you've done it! You've put my eye out! But, by God, you won't do it again!'

When I heard him talking, I closed the door and went to bed, and I said to myself that I wouldn't get up again though he were to break every door in the hotel! The other men were outside. Not one of them would come near the bothy until Anderson had gone away; that was what was keeping them outside. They went off with him then and took him home. My word, he was fairly threatening me! that I'd pay for the blow!

That was Saturday; the next Saturday, he came for me. I had been up at the station in the shop. When I was going up the stairs, oh, I heard talking going on up in the room before me. Who was just before me but Anderson, and one of the lads who was driving for ourselves, Duncan McColl. Anderson was well away, too. I only took a look at him, and went down to our own room, where I used to sleep. He looked at me, and when I had gone down, he turned to McColl.

'A-a-a-h,' he said, 'that's the devil who put my eye out on Saturday night."

'It is,' said McColl.

'A-a-a-h,' said Anderson, 'doesn't he look like a devil?'

'Oh, that's what he is,' said McColl, 'a devil.'

'S-h-h-h, don't say a word. I'm off.'

'I'm sure that's the best thing for you,' said McColl.

'S-h-h! Don't say a word!'

Anderson got up and went out. I went up after a moment. Only McColl was there, bursting with laughter.

'Where's Anderson?' I said.

"It seems Anderson's fled for his life,' he said, 'with the fear he's got of you, when he saw you coming.'

'He didn't need to,' I said. Anderson was slinking before me ever afterwards!

Anderson and the Jar of Whisky

This Anderson, he was refused drink, Fraser wouldn't give him a drop. He went and sent to Glasgow for a jar of whisky. It came on the train to the station. It was a stone jar. Anderson went this evening up to the station to get it. He got hold of the ears of the jar and went off along the road so that everyone could see he had it now, in spite of Fraser! But that wasn't enough for him, but when he was going past the hotel, he had to go in, and show it to Fraser, show him he had now got it in spite of him, and 'you can keep your whisky!'

Fraser was in the bar when Anderson came in.

'Look at that, Mr Fraser! I've got it now, you can keep your own whisky!'

The jar slipped from his hand and broke into pieces behind the counter on the cement. Fraser clapped his hands. Anderson was looking at it, and nearly crying. Every drop was on the floor. Fraser would have preferred what had happened to fifteen pounds! Then he went and handed Anderson a bottle of whisky. 'Go home with that now,' he said, 'if you had been right, you wouldn't have needed to send for that.' Anderson had simply done it to spite him!

The Tramp at Dalmally

There was a lad from Canna called Donald MacLeod who was working along with me for Duncan Fraser the hotel-keeper at Dalmally. One autumn evening we were in the

stable cleaning the horses, and the driver and the guard of
the four-in-hand were in the stable;[6] there were five of us
there. An old man came down from the hotel with a jug of
tea and a piece in his hand. He looked terribly old, his head
was as white as wool. He came into the stable and said the
mistress had sent him down, she had told him there was a bed
in the barn and we would show it to him.

'Oh,' said the driver of the four-in-hand, a man called
James Smith, 'go and show him the bed, Angus.'

I went out. There was a little room inside the door of the
barn. It was there that the bed was; people who were working
there by the day used to be put there to sleep. The bedclothes
were on it and everything. I opened the door myself and
showed him the bed.

'Well,' I said, 'that's your room and your bed. All you have
to do now is to get into it.'

He thanked me very much. I went back into the stable. A
short time after I went into the stable we saw a big red-headed
man come past. He stopped for a moment outside the stable
door and looked in, and went past to the door of the barn. He
had two jackets on, and the one underneath was longer than
the other. Oh, a big red-headed man, his head was as big as a
pot! He went into the barn, but, my goodness! it wasn't long
before the old man came out crying. The fellow who had
come to the barn had taken his food and his tea away from
him.

My word, when I saw that poor old man crying, I felt so
sorry, it left my heart sore.

'Oh, off you go,' said James Smith, 'and kick the rascal out.
You're not worth your porridge, if you're going to let him
stay inside there.'

Donald MacLeod and I went off, with another fellow, one
of the station staff, a man called Neil Leitch. When we got
out, the red-headed man was in the bed. He had thrown the
mug in which the tea had been, down in the middle of the
barn, and was eating the last of the old man's food. Donald
MacLeod and Neil Leitch stood in the door and said to me,
'You go and speak to him, Angus.' I went in.

'What are you doing here?' I said.

'What's it to you what I'm doing here?'

Well, I thought from the way he answered so smartly that he must be working there.

'Are you working on this farm?' I said.

'I am,' he said.

'When did you come here?'

'Yesterday.'

I hadn't been at home yesterday, I had been at Loch Awe.

'Well, surely to God,' I said, 'if you're working here, you could get enough food without taking away from the poor old man what he'd got for himself.'

'He's a liar. I didn't take the food from him.'

'What are you chewing there?' I said.

'I'm not chewing anything that belongs to you,' he said.

'Take care you're telling the truth,' I said, 'or else clear out of here as quick as you ever did, or it'll be the worse for you.'

'I won't,' he said, 'but you will,' and he jumped up; but when he saw the pair at the door, he lay down where he was already. I turned off. 'Well,' I said, 'it's no good for us to trouble him if he's working here; it's likely he's as much right to be here as we have ourselves.'

We returned to the stable. James Smith asked, 'Did you put him out?'

'No, we didn't,' I said. 'He says he's working on the farm here.'

'Oh, I don't believe he is; if he is, we didn't see him.'

'I didn't see him either,' I said, 'but he might be working here without my knowing it, he said he came here yesterday.'

'Oh, indeed, I don't believe he did,' said James.

'Ah, well,' I said, 'it's likely it won't be long before we find out, anyway.'

We went to our supper. When the old man saw that we had not put the red-headed man out, he went back to the hotel (our stable was a bit down from the hotel, but the hotel stable was beside the hotel). He told the mistress what had happened to him. She went and gave him more tea then, and put him into one of the tap-rooms to take it. When we arrived she met us in the passage as we came in.

'Did you see a man down around the barn, Angus?' she said.

'Yes,' I said, 'we saw a man like a tramp down there in the bed in the barn.'

'Oh, for goodness sake, clear him off out of there before he sets the farm on fire.'

'He told me he was working on the farm,' I said.

'Oh, the dirty liar! he isn't, he isn't! Get him away at once!'

'Oh, well then, we'll get him away when we've had our supper.'

We went in to our supper. We were talking about the best plan that might be made to get the tramp away. When we had had our supper, the three of us went back down.

'Go you now,' said Donald MacLeod, 'in where he is, as it was you who was speaking to him before. Don't be afraid of him at all; let him lift a hand to you and devil a bone of him will come out of the barn door whole!'

I went and got a willow switch, and I went in. There he was with the bedclothes around his head. All I did was to catch hold of the bedclothes and pull off every stitch of them and throw them down in the barn. He was naked without a shirt or anything. He got the first stroke right across his body. 'Get up, now, you rascal!' I said, 'and clear out of here.'

He jumped on the bed and landed face down. He didn't say a word, but let out a yell. He got another stroke; he didn't move! When I saw how obstinate he was, I gave him a third stroke along his back; he jumped out of bed then and rushed outside naked between the other two! I went and got a pitchfork and put out the rags he had had on and threw them out after him.

'Get off now!' I said, 'and get dressed and clear off.' He didn't say a word; he began to get dressed, and the poor old man was put into the bed where he had been before. When the tramp had put on these rags, he went off, when he got out to the main road. Heaven help me, but his language! Anyone else would have been disgusted to say what he was saying.

'Oh, clear off,' I said, 'or else if you don't mind what you've got, you'll get more!'

He went off up the road out of our sight. We thought we would stay down at the stable until we gave the horses their supper. There was a little room off the stable loft above the cart shed; we went up there until it was near eight o'clock so that we wouldn't be going back down (from the hotel) again. We were sitting talking there; well, we heard a squeal from the old man down in the stable. We went along; the tramp had come back again and had put the old man out!

'Well, by God,' I said, 'I don't know what we'll do to him. I haven't the heart to give him more than he's had—even though he were a horse!' I was telling the truth—the man was naked.

'I'll tell you what we'll do with him,' said Leitch. 'I'll go and find the policeman and he'll take care of him. It's a risk to be leaving the man there, when we don't know if he won't have set the place on fire by tomorrow.'

'Off with you, then,' I said.

He went off, and he hadn't been gone long when he came with the policeman. The policeman came into the stable.

'Where's the man you've failed to put out?' he said.

'We didn't fail to put him out at all,' I said, 'but he came back again.'

'Where is he?'

'He's out there in the barn.'

'Come along with me, then.'

'Oh, go ahead,' I said. 'You'll get help if you can't do the job yourself.'

He went in. The tramp was stretched out in the bed with the bedclothes around his head. The policeman bent over him and stripped the bedclothes off his head, and looked at him for a while. Then he gave him a tap on the head with his cane. 'Get up out of there.' The fellow didn't say a word; he didn't move. The policeman gave him another tap. 'Get up out of there, you!' He didn't move. 'Get up,' said the policeman, 'or else I'll break the cane on your head.'

Then the tramp got up. He tried to go off naked as he had done before. The policeman stood in his way. 'Put your clothes on!' He began to put his clothes on. Upon my soul, he took a good time! 'On you go, now,' said the policeman, 'walk ahead of me.' He went off handcuffed. The policeman asked him to hold out his hands. He held out his hands at once. He knew that it was just as well for him to do so.

The policeman went off with him. This was on Saturday night. On Sunday, when we were at our breakfast—we didn't get our breakfast on Sunday until nine o'clock—what did I see but the policeman walking outside in front of the window. He asked the first of the lads who went out if I were inside there. The fellow said I was.

'Go and tell him to come out,' said the policeman.

The other fellow came in. 'The policeman's wanting you, Angus,' he said. I went out. He started questioning me about the old man, had I seen the tramp taking the food from him?

'I didn't see the tramp taking the food from him,' I said; 'it was what the old man said he did.'

'Wasn't he eating when you went in?'

'He was chewing, but I don't know what he was swallowing.'

The policeman began to laugh.

'Have you got him yet?' I said.

'Yes, and I'll keep him until I take him to Oban on Monday morning.'

'My word, aren't you hard up for a case! Go and let him out and give him three kicks on the way!'

'Oh, it won't do for me to do that; I'm sure you saw him taking the old man's food away.'

'I didn't see him take the food away. I don't care what you do, but don't bring me into it.'

'Tut! Be quiet. Wouldn't you like a day's holiday down there?'

'Some holiday,' I said, 'going to give evidence against a tramp! I wouldn't do it for all my wages! You should know me better than that!' (The policeman was a North Uist man.)

'Oh, well, he'll likely admit it.'

'I don't care whether he does or not,' I said. 'but I'd much sooner you'd let him go.'

'Didn't you hear about the man who broke into the house up at Glenorchy? There was only an old woman and a young girl there—five weeks ago, the house was robbed and neither of them dared to go outside the door?'

'I heard of it,' I said, 'but goodness knows where that man is today.'

'That's him,' the policeman said. 'It's a long time since I got information about him and I'm very glad I've got him. Are you asking me now to let the fellow go?'

'Oh, be off with you, for goodness sake,' I said, 'that's enough!'

The policeman took him to Oban on the Monday, and he got six months' imprisonment for robbing the house and taking everything in it. That's what happened to the tramp who came our way!

How I Left Dalmally

When I was working for Duncan Fraser at Dalmally, he was as kind a master as I ever was with. The first year I worked for him, I wanted to go home for the winter, as only my father and mother were at home. Well, he asked me if I would come back again at the beginning of the summer, and I said I didn't know, that if my father and mother were keeping middling well, I would. 'But I don't want—I'm unwilling—it's time for me to stop working with horses.'

'Would you be willing to go as a ghillie down at the Loch Awe Hotel?' he said. (He had the Loch Awe Hotel as well as the Dalmally Hotel, he owned it outright.)

'I would,' I said. 'That's something that would suit me fine.'

'Very well then, leave your address, and we'll be hearing from you.'

I came home for the whole winter. But at the beginning of spring I got a letter from him to come out. Well, I knew there was nothing to be done at Loch Awe at that time of year, that there would be nothing until after St Patrick's Day anyway, when fishermen would be coming. I was at work myself ploughing at home. I wrote back to him and said that I couldn't come sooner than the beginning of April. I got another letter from him asking me to be sure to come on then, that the situation was awaiting me.

I didn't hear from him again, neither did I write to him, but I went at the end of spring. When I reached Loch Awe, I put my trunk off at Loch Awe, at the station, and went up to Dalmally, he was staying at the other hotel. I only saw him that night through the window of the bar, with two of the tourists along with him. Next morning he came out.

'I hope you'll excuse me, Angus, I didn't manage to come to you yesterday, but I saw you through the window. There were two gentlemen with me at the time.'

He asked me how I had left them at home, and I said that they were well enough when I left them. He hadn't got anyone in my place, he had only one fellow, a lad from Perth.

'Well,' he said, 'would you be willing, Angus, to stay here a day or two to get the potatoes planted? Alec's all by himself.'

'My clothes are down at Loch Awe, I put my trunk off at Loch Awe.'

'Oh, I'll bring it up when I come in the evening.'

Well, that was all right. I went and stripped and began working along with the other fellow, putting out manure, cleaning the land. I was there all the week, and I never heard a word about getting to Loch Awe. The next week came; no word of it.

'Oh, damn it,' I said, turning to the other fellow, 'what does he mean, isn't he going to get another man here along with you in my place?'

'Well, I often spoke to him about it since winter came, and every time I spoke to him, he would say "Angus is coming next week". When I heard that Angus was coming, I was as happy as if the work had been finished. Angus didn't come till now!'

'Well, it wasn't to stay along with you that Angus came this year at all.'

'Ah, well,' he said, 'I wouldn't ask him for that, but I don't know that you wouldn't be as well off where you are, than if you went to Loch Awe.'

'Oh, I don't know, I'm tired enough of it.'

But at last the term-day was nearly on us, and there wasn't a word about Loch Awe. I was then watching the newspaper, and I saw there a man over at Colintraive, a hotelkeeper, called

James MacLellan, wanting a ferryman and an assistant on the pier. I went and put in for that job. Oh, I got a letter from him at once asking me to go, and telling me the wage, that fourteen pounds (in the half-year) was the highest wages he was paying a ferryman, but that I'd have a bit of a chance (of getting tips) and that I would get one Sunday off in the month, that Sunday was as busy a day as any for the ferry. Well, it was humiliating for me to go for fourteen pounds, when I was getting more than that where I was. I told him that if I would get fifteen pounds (in the half-year) I would go, but if I wouldn't, I wouldn't go at all. I never heard another word from him. The job was advertised in the newspaper the next week.

But then I saw that a doctor was wanting a driver up at Roy Bridge, he was paying a pound a week, 'board and lodgings' and the driver would only have to drive him, and do a little work in the garden. My word, I said to myself that this was better. I put in for it. You had to have a good character. I told him that if he needed a character, to write to my master, Duncan Fraser, Dalmally Hotel, that he would get my character there. I didn't get a reply at all.

But more than a week later, the boss was going past while I was working in the field. He stopped at the gate, with a letter in his hand. He called to me, 'There's a letter for you here; there's no reason for me to bring you to the house at all.'

'You don't indeed.'

Who was the letter from but the doctor! miscalling me for having put in for the job when I was engaged where I was. He'd let me see that I'd stop making fun of him! I didn't know what in the world to say. The other fellow was there, and he asked me:

'Is it from the doctor, Angus?'

'It is,' I said.

'Did you get the job?'

'Indeed, no, he was threatening me with the law.'

'Why was that?'

'I don't know.'

I went and handed him the letter. He read it and began to laugh.

'Oh, he's done to you just what he did to a barmaid he had up here for a year. She put in for a place like that; a letter came asking for a reference. He replied that she wasn't leaving at all, that he had her under engagement. The girl wasn't under an engagement at all, but he didn't let her away for all that.'

'Well, the son of perdition,' I said, 'he won't do it to me. If I've time to send the doctor a wire after we stop work, I'll send it.'

'I think you'll manage to do it like that. If there isn't time you'd probably get it away first thing tomorrow; you won't get one away tonight any more anyway.'

We went in to our supper. We sat down at the table; it was just three days before the term, before Whitsuntide. The barmaid came up behind me.

'The boss wants to see you, Angus, when you've had your supper.'

'Very good,' I said.

When I had had my supper, I got up and went along. I asked the barmaid where he was. 'He's in the sitting-room,' she said. I went in. He and his wife and two daughters were there, and the manager. There was a table there covered with banknotes, and an iron box with a partition in the middle, and one end of it was full of silver and the other was full of sovereigns.

'Sit down, Angus,' he said, 'sit down. The term is getting near, lads, and I'm sure you'd like money, if there's a penny left today.'

'If I get what's left,' I said, 'I'll be pleased enough.'

The boss began to laugh. 'And,' he said, 'what do you say to me about staying on here now for another six months, Angus?'

'Well, it wasn't to stay here that I came this year at all.'

'I know that,' he said. 'But I'd have let you go to Loch Awe long ago, if there had been anything doing there; but the men at Loch Awe are only leaning against the wall, and I know that if you went there, you wouldn't be happy there, and indeed I wouldn't like to let you go to a place where you wouldn't be happy.'

'Well, I'm not happy where I am.'

'What have you got against it? Tell me; if it can be put right, we'll put it right.'

'Well, I've had one thing against it,' I said, 'the number of times I've had to leave my own work and perhaps go off with a hire to Inveraray. And my work was only standing there until I got back to it.'

'Didn't the loss fall on me?' he said.

'No doubt it did,' I said, 'but the trouble fell on us.'

'Oh, I see that,' he said. 'I see that you were exhausting yourselves working until eight or nine o'clock; but all the same it wouldn't be right for me to forget that; but have you anything against your sleeping quarters?'

'Indeed, no,' I said, 'the Prince of Wales could sleep in my bed.'

'Well, I'm pleased to hear that. Have you anything against your food?'

'Indeed, I have not, nothing against any of it.'

'Well, I'm very glad,' he said. 'Well, I got a letter all right from that big doctor asking for your reference; I understand you were putting in for another place."

'I was,' I said, 'but I know it was you that kept it from me.'

'I didn't keep it from you at all,' he said. 'I'd be very sorry to keep anything good from you; but I got a letter indeed from that big doctor, and he asked for your reference; and I sent word back to him that I wasn't going to part with you. I couldn't give you a better reference than that.'

'Oh, that's good enough,' I said, 'but I'm not going to stay.'

'Well, then, Angus, if that's what's coming between us, I'll let you go to Loch Awe tomorrow morning, but I know you won't be happy there; and if you take my advice, it'll be better for you to stay where you are for another six months. What wages did you have last year?'

'Fifteen pounds,' I said.[10]

'Well, we can raise your wages. You'll get another pound. Will that satisfy you?'

'It won't.'

'Would you like more?'

175

'Well, I don't know who wouldn't like more,' I said.

'And what do you say yourself?'

'I don't know,' I said, 'but I'll not stay for less than seventeen pounds anyway.' I didn't expect that he'd give me that.

'Well, Angus,' he said, 'seventeen pounds is a big wage, but for a pound or two more, for a right lad, I've nothing to say about it. You'll get what you're asking.'

'Oh, well,' I said, catching hold of something, 'an engagement[11] won't do for me any more. There's only my father and mother at home, and perhaps I'll have to go home at half term, and that wouldn't suit you.'

'I've nothing against that, Angus,' he said. 'I'll let you away to go home any time though you were engaged for a year; but I'm not for letting you go to another man any day I can pay you as much as the other man would."

'Oh, well, well, then,' I said, 'leave it at that.'

He was just as happy as a king!

'Well, now,' he said, 'how long is it since you came, then?'

'It's eight weeks from last Monday.'

He took his book. 'It is, just,' he said. 'Nine weeks from next Monday.'

'That Monday hasn't come yet,' I said.

'Oh, well, it hasn't,' he said, 'but as for a day or two, we aren't going to break the week on you. You'll now get the wages the doctor was going to give you, then, for the time since you came. You'll get a pound a week. Are you happy now?'

'Oh indeed I am.'

'Well, I'd like to make you happy,' he said.

When I left him, the day I left him, I had to stay a week after the term to let the other fellow away for his holidays, as I was going home. He was as fine a master as I ever had!

7

SOUTH UIST AGAIN

At the Fishing

THEN MY father got a croft from the Congested Districts
Board, and I came home, and helped my father work the croft,
and started at the fishing. I got a boat, and my neighbour John
MacAskill and another man John MacDonald, and I, worked
together steady. We fished herring and mackerel, ling and cod
and lobsters and every kind of fishing. Sometimes we were
doing very well, and sometimes we were working at a loss.
Often we were in danger of losing our lives. One night Mac-
Askill and I were out by ourselves in a little boat, sixteen feet
long, and it came on bad at sea. We tried to get into an an-
chorage where we could shelter. When we were only twenty
yards outside, it came on a hurricane against us, and we were
likely to be blown out to the open sea. We were going past a
promontory and staying as close to the shore as we could, and
we managed to put down an anchor as we went past the point
of the promontory. The anchor held, and we managed to put
another out. We sat in the boat all the winter night, and
neither of us could see the other for spindrift. That was the
longest night I ever spent.

I used to be out fishing steady, and often awake all night.
One time my neighbour Johnny MacAskill and I, had been at
Lochboisdale. It was very calm—it was the beginning of
summer—and we were rowing back and forward.

There is a bad place in Loch Eynort where there is a tidal
current—the 'Sruth Beag' or 'Little Current' it's called—
which runs at seven knots at spring tides. When we arrived

from Lochboisdale, the current was so strong we could not get into Loch Eynort against it. There is a submerged rock outside the place where the current runs into the sea. We let out our anchor at the outside end of this rock, to wait until the current would slacken at low tide. We had a lot of meal and salt aboard. We were tired out, and we stretched out and fell asleep. Johnny MacAskill was sleeping below aft, and I was lying amidships. When I awoke, my two feet were above my head as if I were upside down against a wall. I looked around, and saw that the sea was up to the gunwale and just about to come in amidships; the boat had gone dry on the middle of the submerged rock (with the falling tide) and was about to turn upside down around our heads! Things looked ugly.

Johnny MacAskill was lying below aft on the other side of the boat, and was now standing straight up against her side! I was too frightened to say anything. I got up and began to crawl up the high side of her. The anchor was high up on the gunwale. I managed to reach it and to throw it out on the rock, and I let myself on to the rock holding on to the anchor rope and threw the anchor behind the rock, and I managed to tie the rope to the boat's tholepins and made it as tight as I could so that the boat would stay the way she was, and then I woke Johnny MacAskill up. When he opened his eyes, 'God save me,' he said, 'where are we?'

'Never mind where you are,' I said, 'but see you get out of her before she turns upside down over your head.' He dragged himself out of her on to the rock, and we held her there. Luckily it was just low tide. Well, we kept her from turning over with the anchor until the tide came in and raised her. The sea was up to the top of our knees above the rock before she floated on an even keel. Then we got out of her and came home. The sun had risen, and we were glad to have escaped from the danger in which we had been. I never saw such a miracle as when the boat stayed on top of the rock and didn't turn upside down over us!

Another time I and two of my brothers and Johnny MacAskill were setting nets for herring. We heard that herring were being got in Lochboisdale, and this day we were on our way there. Half-way, at a place called Stuley

Island, it came on very bad against us. We had only a small boat, sixteen feet long. I went to take down the sail, and the first seas she took in over the bow went over my head, and didn't leave the breadth of a penny dry on me until it ran out of my boots.

We turned back there, and when we came into Loch Eynort, it turned into a north-west gale against us. We took shelter there, and stayed there to keep the boat safe, there was no way for us to land. Night was coming on, and it was so dark that I couldn't see the man who was in her bow. There I was, dripping wet; the others were all right, they had oilskins on at the time, but I didn't have oilskins on at all. The water that was going on my back, was running down to my boots. What I did then was to take off my shirt and my underclothes, to try to wring them out. I put an oilskin on while I was wringing out my underclothes, and indeed, it wasn't warm! Then I put my underclothes on again, and my shirt, and put on the oilskin over them; and I was sitting in the boat dressed like this until day broke, and when day broke, the wind was so strong that we couldn't bring the boat up the loch, but we got ashore, and were going to walk in to the houses. We had more than three miles to walk.

After I got ashore, I couldn't walk, my knees wouldn't bend at all. I sat down then on a stone, and began to rub my legs. I'm sure I spent half an hour rubbing them before I could manage to bend them. Then I tried to walk, and I was falling my length as often as I was standing! But I became more supple, and was able to walk well enough, and we got to the houses. I didn't expect to do a turn ever afterwards, but I didn't even catch a cold, though I've caught many a cold since then, for very little reason. I got over that trial very well.

I remember two years that the herrings came into Loch Eynort. They were so plentiful that the loch was dry; they were so plentiful that when the tide ebbed, the shore looked white with them; they were very good herring, and there was nothing for them. Boats were catching them and taking them away to Mallaig. We were only working with small boats; we were working inside the loch. It didn't matter where we set the nets, the loch was full of herring all winter and spring, until the end of spring. That was (nearly) forty years ago, the year after the war began, just, the first war, the first year it was on. Well, the herring was there again two years later. I never saw it come in again to the loch so plentiful, but it was coming into the mouth of the loch often enough. There was no price for it, seven shillings a cran, and five shillings a cran; it was better than nothing, that's all there was to it.

We had plenty of it salted, and everyone in the district down here had plenty. We were dumping it in the sea at last. Then we stopped fishing for it, there was no use in being at it.

We used to get cod with lines. It was very few flounders that we caught, we weren't setting small lines for flounders at all, but great lines for cod and ling. We had five or six baskets of lines, with a hundred hooks on each line. We used to set them when sailing; but there was need for two pretty handy fellows to be at it, one to bait the lines, and the other to set them; indeed, he didn't need to make a mistake; if he were to lift the wrong hook, the whole basket would get entangled.

There wasn't much doing with the lobsters. If they had been fetching the kind of price they are today—but it was seven shillings a dozen that we were getting for them. Donald Ferguson was buying them, and buying the fish, no one here was buying but himself. He had the district to himself. I remember when the East Coast men were coming here too, he used to buy their fish too; they themselves used to salt them and fillet them, and he used to buy them and dry them, and send them away then to sell. That's the way he used to work.

Fishing was hard work, cold work, and often dangerous work too.

One night I lost seven nets in the mouth of the loch, with herring. We had set nine nets, and could only lift two of them. They had gone straight to the bottom like stones. I am sure there was twenty crans in each net. You couldn't see the nets at all, they were just one white lump altogether. We lost seven nets there that night. It was enough for us to take the two nets aboard; there were seven of us pulling those two nets; seven of us. We lost the others.

I used to fish lobsters out on the west side. You had to go a good way away from the shore there before you found much depth, before you came to twenty fathoms depth. We used to go so far out to the west that we could see the east side, the mouth of Loch Eynort; we couldn't see the low land at all. Well now, there was only twenty-five fathoms depth there. It was out there that we used to get the lobsters at the beginning of summer, none were caught in at the shore early in the year, early in summer. What were caught, were in the open sea. When they came into the shore, into shallow water, it wasn't necessary to go as far out as that, it wasn't.

We used to take the boat in around Eriskay Sound, or through the Benbecula sea-fords. If it was a good day and the wind was favourable, it didn't take long to go around at all. We had forty to sixty creels. It was Donald Ferguson who was buying the lobsters, and we used to be getting things in his shop. There was nothing a fisherman needed that Donald Ferguson didn't have. Nets, lines, twine for lobster creels, whatever you wanted, you would get there. He used to engage the boats for the summer and the first month of autumn. You would get seven shillings a dozen for the lobsters; well, a little more than that during winter, when they had become scarce; then he was giving eight shillings a dozen for them, sometimes nine shillings. But they had to be four inches long in the chest, before they could count as whole lobsters; if they were smaller than that, he only counted them as half-lobsters; and even if they were a foot long, if they had lost a claw, they only counted as half-lobsters. He was making a fortune for himself.[1]

The creature that gave me the biggest scare I ever had, was a whale. One night in the autumn we were setting nets, out in the head of Loch Eynort. There was plenty of herring, and if there was, there was plenty after it; there were whales after it, and the sea was just full of dogfish. Well, they began to set the nets. The whale surfaced beside our boat, and the buoy I was throwing out struck her on her side. She stayed on the surface; she was as long as the net, and her two eyes were nearly as big as that chair, and she was so black! I had no doubt whatever that she wouldn't come under the boat. Oh, she didn't trouble us at all, she was a while on the surface and then she just quietly submerged, and I didn't see her again. But she frightened us enough, indeed! She was as long as a

herring net, eighteen fathoms; that much of her was on the
surface, from buoy to buoy. I struck her with a buoy on the
side; she paid no heed. She was the biggest one I ever saw.
But, indeed, we were very happy that she went away, that
she cleared off.

Fr John Mackintosh and the Wild Duck

One winter night Johnny MacAskill and I went hunting.
There was snow on the ground. We went into Kildonan.
Down on the Rodha[2] there, on the shore, there were many
wild ducks coming in there when there was snow and frost,
looking for fresh water; that was where we were going. When
we reached Kildonan, it hadn't got rightly dark. The farmer
had a stack-yard down by the river with stacks of hay in it, a
dozen stacks. We went into the stack-yard amongst the
stacks, until it should get dark.

My word, then we saw a flock of ducks coming, and oh!
they settled just below the Rodha in the fresh water. We were
delighted, but what the pity did we see but two men coming
round stealthily down by the shore on the other side of
the fresh water, with dogs stalking after them. My word, this
was the gamekeepers; but how were we to get away, or
escape?

I had a big black white-necked dog, which I had got from
Fr John Mackintosh as a puppy, it was a very good gun-dog.
We waited in the stack-yard for it to get dark so they mightn't
see us, if we could get to escape. But they got a chance at
the duck and let off four tremendous shots. Our dogs jumped
out over the wall down to the shore, and all they did was to
jump out over the other side (of the Rodha) and make for
Aird Mhaoile northwards on the 'machair'. We thought they
were after us, and we expected to hear any moment shots
being fired at our dogs; but we didn't.

But then the black dog caught up with us down on the
'machair' with a wild duck in his mouth.

'Go on, my lad,' said Johnny, 'you got your share from the
battle!'

We kept on down to the point of Aird Mhaoile; we didn't

dare to fire a shot in case we couldn't get clear of the 'machair'
before they traced us. We went on up to Bornish[3] and when
we were along there, towards the road to the church there—
John Ferguson the farmer had a compost-heap at the head of
the Rodha, and what the pity did we see but these two men
coming towards us up beside the loch! We had nowhere to
hide, but we went to the compost-mound. The two men made
straight for the compost-mound! Then we heard Fr John
Mackintosh speak:

'Is anyone here?' he said.

It was then that we recognized who it was. Who on earth
was it but Fr John and the son of Rory the son of Young
Donald! and they had gone to the foot of the Rodha! Then
he asked us.

'Wasn't it you that was up at the Rodha?'

'It was,' I said.

'God preserve me!' he said. 'Why didn't you come down
where we were?'

'We thought you were the gamekeepers,' I said.

'We thought you were the gamekeepers yourselves,' he said,
'your dogs were quicker out than our own ones. The first
living thing your dog got hold of, he didn't come to us with it,
but he made off in the other direction, and we never got
another sight of it. But you spoiled our sport, and we spoilt
yours.'

They hadn't got anything, they had only three wild ducks.
They didn't get anything but what they had got at that
moment. We offered them the duck which the black dog
brought back, but they wouldn't take it. 'Take it home
with you.' That's what happened to us that night, we didn't
get much, anyway.

The King Otter

One night I and my neighbour Alasdair MacDonald,
Alasdair the son of John in Loch Eynort, went hunting at night.
There was a beautiful moon, and snow. We went out there to
the brae of Ormaclate, where the Ormaclate peat is, out on the
moor. There was a canal there between two lochs, and the

wild geese used to lie there, and ducks, when there was snow and frost.

When we got there there was neither goose nor duck there. We sat down at the foot of a knoll there; there was a kind of a loch at the end of the canal there, and it was open. That was where the wild ducks used to come to get water when it was freezing. I went down beside the loch to see if I could find a stone to sit on in the snow without getting wet. There was a little stone ruin at the edge of the loch, I think it was a place where they used to make whisky, it looked like that.

Every stone I tried was frozen so hard (I couldn't move it). But then this head appeared outside the ruin when I was inside, not six paces away from me. I went straight in carefully; I might have put my hand on it outside the ruin. It stood there looking at me, and—well, I thought it was an otter, but it was big. It came out of the water all but its tail —its tail was in the water. I retreated—I couldn't say a word —to try to get Alasdair, who was sitting above me, to give me the gun. I began to beckon with my hand behind me—my head was bent down—and he understood that I was seeing something; but he didn't see anything, the ruin was between him and the otter.

He went and took the gun and crept down and stretched it out to me behind me. I got the gun. There were two cartridges in it—it was a muzzle-loader, too. Well, when I had caught hold of the gun, I had to back three paces, the otter was so close to me I couldn't lift the gun to it. I lifted the gun, and tried the right barrel; it didn't go off. Immediately I tried the other barrel; it didn't go off. I thought the gun had got wet, and I threw away the caps and put two fresh caps on it. I lifted it again, and pulled the trigger twice in succession; it didn't go off. The hammer made a click on the caps as if it were hitting an iron bar.

'Oh, damn it all!' I said 'everything's soaked.' I turned away. The otter just backed quietly away as it had come in.

'What were you snapping at there?' said Alasdair.

'Wasn't it an otter?' I said.

'Where was it?'

'In front of me, below the ruin.'

'Ah, it wasn't an otter!'

'Well, I thought it was an otter, anyway,' I said.

'No; it must have been a witch!'

'Well, if I had thought of that I would have put silver in the gun. But whatever it was, we may as well go home, everything there is must be soaked.'

But just at that moment there came a wild duck and drake, and they settled just in front of us in the moonlight.

'Have you got a cartridge in the gun?' I said.

'I have not,' said Alasdair. 'Won't you try at them?'

'What's the use of me trying at them,' I said, 'when it refused to fire four times?'

'I don't know; won't you try at them?'

I went and lifted the gun as he suggested and tried a shot at them, and killed them both! The second barrel fired just as quickly. Then it occurred to me, what on earth had I been pulling the trigger at when neither cap nor anything else would fire? Whatever it was, I wasn't afraid of it, but it astonished me that the cartridge wouldn't fire at it, it must have been something uncanny!

I had a brother-in-law who was a long time a shepherd in Tiree, who had a gun, and used to go out with it at times. One day he went down to the shore, and saw an otter coming ashore. He got between it and the sea, and it went in below a big stone in the bank of the beach. He had a good chance at it, he was up towards the stone, and the otter was looking at him from under the rock. He fired at it, and the otter was as alive as ever. He fired again. The otter was still alive watching him. He stood between it and the sea, and it couldn't escape.

He fired seven shots at it; and it was with his stick that he killed it at last, and he said, that if there ever had been a King Otter, this was it. When he was skinning it, he was taking the lead out of its hair with his fingers, not one grain of shot had even gone through, the shot was sticking in its bristles![4]

Alasdair Mór the Storyteller and the Storm

One night Allan MacMillan and I went to see Alasdair Mór. There was a sheiling out there at a place called Haun, there was a cove where the fishermen used to come in with their boats. We came in there, and we were going to stay in the sheiling; we only had a small boat. When we arrived, there was no roof on the sheiling. There was nothing better, the night being what it was, than to make for Alasdair Mór's house. We left the boat there (in the cove) and the nets set.

Alasdair's house was at the foot of a cliff and though it was blowing a gale, if you were inside you wouldn't know the wind was blowing at all. What happened but the wind veered, and blew a gale from the south and the south-east against the shore. We thought it was a perfect night and all we heard was Alasdair's yarns and stories.[5] We were enjoying ourselves exceedingly.

When it got light there, we felt the wind blowing strongly when we came out of Alasdair Mór's house. I could not keep my cap on my head with the storm. When we came over to where we had left the boat we found the boat had filled up and had sunk. We didn't know what in the world we should do. The oars and the sail and the mast were up on the shore. We thought that she had been spoilt and holed, and that we were just done for. We couldn't see the nets at all, there was no sign of them, they had been pulled out into deep water, with the north-westerly gale.

But at any rate we managed to refloat the boat and to bring it ashore. It was undamaged and safe enough. We got everything into it. The anchors—our nets were anchored—had caught on a submerged rock some way out from the end of the loch. We got the nets safely but there was nothing in them. We were fed up with the stories of Alasdair Mór! We had paid for them all right when we got home after refloating the boat and recovering the nets!

Alasdair Mór and the Hoggs

Once I and Alasdair MacDonald and Allan MacMillan were setting nets for herring in the winter. The night was fine and when we had set the net at the mouth of Loch Eynort,[6] there was nothing better to do than to take the boat into a safe place

and anchor her, and we would go over the hill to Alasdair
Mór's house, which was behind the hill, behind Benmore.

This we did, and when we arrived Alasdair and his wife
and one or two of his children were at home. Alasdair made us
very welcome and began telling stories and romances. He
didn't go to bed all night, but was telling stories about this
person and that and about things that had happened to himself and how the farm manager was trying to catch him out,
and that sort of thing. The farm manager, a man called Mac-
Donald, who was then in Ormaclate was a very hard fellow.
Ranald MacDonald, who then was tenant of Ormaclate, had
sent home fifty hoggs, and the manager had made Alasdair
take them out to behind Benmore, and had said to him that
if he brought them all in at Whitsuntide, he would get a
pound of tobacco over and above his wages.

'Anyway,' said Alasdair, 'I was seeing them every day. This
time, what happened but I missed one of them; I could find
no trace of her. I went all over the place and couldn't get her;
she must have fallen down on the shore. Ah, there was no help
for it; it seems likely I wouldn't get the pound of tobacco,'
said Alasdair, 'when I lost the hogg. Then I got word to bring
them into Ormaclate. I went and got hold of the shaggiest
hogg that was most like them in Ormaclate, and I put the
same keel-mark on her that was on the others, and I took her
with me. When I arrived I put them into a shed and I went
into the house. When the manager came down, he said:

'You've arrived, Alasdair!'

'I have,' I said.

'Have you brought in the hoggs?'

'I have.'

'Have you got them all?'

'I have."

'Let's go and see them, then.'

We went out then. The manager was going through them
inspecting them.

'Well, I don't think yon's one of them at all, Alasdair,' he said.

'She's one of them all right,' I said. 'Hasn't she got the
same keel-mark on her as the others?'

'Oh, keel will stick to any fleece, Alasdair!'

'Oh, you're only saying that to keep the pound of tobacco from me; you must give it to me, though it hurts your guts.'

Well, I got the pound of tobacco, said Alasdair, but he was very doubtful about her. He was a real rascal. Another time, at lambing time, I got up this morning and it had been raining all night. When I looked out, what did I see but the 'grey manager's' hat going away from me up in Glen Thormasgor above the house. Well, I said to myself that it was high time for me to be off. I only waited to put on my jacket and then I made off as quick as I ever did over to the shore. When I was going by the Tearasdal river I took off my jacket, I wetted it in the stream. I continued on, and he saw me, and came down to where I was.

'You're up, Alasdair!' he said.

'Right enough, it's a while since I got up, and I'm thinking it's a while since you got up too, if you're here now.'

'It's a while since I got up, sure enough, but you've only just got up.'

'"That's what my coat-tail shows,' I said, and I caught hold of my jacket and squeezed it.

'Aye,' he said, 'you're wet.'

'I am wet, indeed.'

'Where have you been?'

'I went out to the Dark Glen.'

'Why, I came out that way and I didn't notice a dog or anything.'

'I didn't need to be working a dog there.'

He came to the house with me, said Alasdair, and I took off my jacket; if he had caught me indoors that day, it would have been the high road for me!

How I Managed to Keep My Sheep

As long as Charles MacLean had the farm of Gearrabhailteas, we had leave to keep some sheep on the hill. I used to work for him. When he gave up the farm, Mr MacDonald came there from Barra. He had had Vatersay.[7] Well, the order was that no one was to have sheep on the place but himself. All the shepherds had some sheep of their own, and they had to get rid of them. My sheep were on the hill, and I would have no chance to keep them unless I got someone else to keep them on his land for me.

Anyway, MacDonald had a shepherd out at Loch Eynort called Christie, and when there was to be a gathering, Christie used to give me a warning to take my sheep off the hill to my house so that they would not be taken into the fank. I used to do this, and MacDonald didn't know I had any sheep on his hill! He had a half-wit of a manager from the Isle of Skye, called Neil Beaton, who was a lot worse than his master, if he got up against you. This time I was sent for to go to shear at Gearrabhailteas. It was the old sheep off the 'machair' we had to shear, and it was difficult to shear them, as some of their fleeces were full of sand. Beaton thought there was no one as good at shearing as himself. This day he came out in good trim; I was sitting on the shearing-stool opposite him. The first sheep he got, he said, 'Get a move on, MacLellan.' I didn't think anything of it, I thought he was joking at first; but when he had shorn the sheep, 'That's one!' he shouted.

'Well, it won't be long before this one's done too,' I said. My sheep was put out, and we got two others, but before he was half-way with his second one, mine was done and away. 'That's two,' I said. 'He'll have to hurry.' Before he had put out his second one, my third one was ready to go along with her.

'Oh,' I said, 'there isn't a man on the island who can beat me at this. You may as well give up now.'

He didn't say a word, but he got so red in the face! He got up and jumped over the shearing-stool. 'Let me see your shears,' he said. 'There they are.' He took hold of them and tried them. 'There isn't a pair like them here,' he said. 'Haven't they fallen into good hands?' I replied. He could only agree.

We were going to finish shearing the old sheep early. Beaton came out and said to Christie 'Go and bring down the ones across the road this side of the hill-top, and the ones around the mill, and we'll have less to do tomorrow.' He turned to me: 'Have you got your dog?' he said.

'No.'

'Why didn't you bring him with you?'

'I didn't need a dog here.'

'Well, you'll have to go to gather in the morning.'

'All right, isn't the dog out there already? Where are you going to gather?'

'The hillside above Loch Eynort,' he said.

My word, when I heard this, I knew my own sheep were out on the hill! Every one of them would be in the fank to-morrow!

I didn't let on, but when Christie was going off, I said to him:

'Don't bring in any more than you can help. Give me a chance to get off early. Put them off to the hill with the dog.'

'I will if I can,' he said.

Christie went off, and came back with two hundred sheep! I could have boiled him when I saw what he had brought in. The sun was getting pretty low. Well, I said to myself that if there was a chance to get away, I would have to go tonight, there would be no use trying to get my sheep in the morning. I began to shear for all I could. Beaton said I had gone mad. The sun had just set by the time we had finished. I asked what time would they be starting to gather.

'Oh, I'm sure they'll only wait till they've taken their food.'

'Well, though you went right away, I'll be there before you.'

'Well!' he said, 'there's steel in MacLellan!'

I didn't make for my house, but for the hill. I got all my sheep in except one, without a dog or anything else to drive them except pieces of turf! I drove them to our house. When I arrived, my mother, peace to her soul, was waiting for me. By then it was one in the morning. I lit the lantern and hung it in the cowshed and put the sheep inside, and shut the door. I had to take off every stitch I had on and put dry clothes on. Everything I had on was soaked with sweat.

When I had had something to eat, all there was for it was to go back to the hill. I was only just sitting down to light my pipe after reaching the top when I heard Beaton's shout from the hillside above me. My dog began to bark. He heard it. 'Ha, there you are!' he said. 'Yes,' I replied, 'you haven't got the better of me yet!'

Having escaped this time, I said to myself that the day would come when he would get the better of me, and that the best thing I could do would be to report my sheep myself, rather than have anyone else do it. I went to Gearrabhailteas. One of the farmer's daughters met me outside. I asked her if her father was in, and she said he was. 'Come in,' she said. I went in. He was in the parlour. She went and brought him.

'Well, my good fellow? What are you doing at Loch Eynort, Angus?'

'Not much.'

'Is that what you've come to see me about?'

'Yes.'

'What is it?'

'A few sheep I've got out on the hill there. If you can't let them stay there—they were born and reared there—I'll have to send them away, I haven't got a place for them myself.'

'Are there many of them?'

'There are twelve ewes with lambs and a few eld sheep with them.'

'Oh, well, Angus, as for that number, it won't make any difference to the hill. Leave them there since they're there.'

'Well,' I said, 'whatever you're asking me for keeping them, I'd be ready to give you.'

'Oh, indeed, you're doing a lot for us. Leave them there.' I got leave to keep the sheep there, when no one else in the township was allowed to keep a single sheep!

Our Dogs in the Dock

In 1907 crofts were made for us at Loch Eynort, for the people originally there. The place had been in the hands of the tacksman before that, and we were only sub-tenants. A new tenant had come to Ormaclate (in 1906), a man from Mull; we wrote then to Lady Cathcart Gordon to ask if the place where we were could be made into crofts for us, if the farmer agreed.

Well, Lady Cathcart Gordon sent word to the Factor to go and see what kind of place the people at Loch Eynort had, and said she thought it was suitable enough to make into crofts if the farmer was willing to part with it. The Factor came out to see the place, and he thought it suitable too. The farmer was willing enough to let them have it; whatever rent was put on it, would be taken off his own. The crofts were made for us then; there were nine families of us then at Loch Eynort.

When we took possession of the crofts, we had to sign for the Factor, that we wouldn't have a dog at all. Some of us signed, every one of us eventually, and plenty of us had no idea what we were putting our names to. When we got together, we put our heads together and saw what we had done—that we mightn't have a dog at all. Well, it wasn't easy for us to do the job without a dog, and particularly it wasn't easy for me, because I had sheep, and I had no way to gather them or to take them to be dipped or anywhere else unless I had a dog.

So we had to write then to the Factor to say we had to get our signatures back, because we didn't know what we were signing at the time. Well, he wrote a letter to us saying he couldn't see what need we had for dogs, but that he would consult Lady Cathcart Gordon and the Congested Districts Board about it.[9] That was all right. But very soon afterwards, we got a summons to go to Lochmaddy because of the dogs, every one of us in the district. We didn't know what in the world we should do, but we had to appear.

Well, we took the steamer north, and the people in the north part of South Uist went by the fords[10]; and the weather was bad at the time too. Many of them were pretty wet before they got to the fords. There was a lawyer of Lochmaddy called MacDonald; we went to see him, and he took our case, and said he would appear on our behalf.

Wilson appeared for Lady Cathcart Gordon, and for the Factor of North Uist, and for the Factor of Harris; the three estates went in together, and it was Wilson who represented them. Wilson was pretty clever. Three crofters went over from Barra from every township, and MacDonald asked for the same from South Uist. Three of us went there from Loch Eynort, and I was one of them. When we arrived, MacDonald took us into his office. He told us to stand fast, that we wouldn't lose our dogs at all.

We told him we had written to the Factor to ask for our signatures back, and that he had sent us a letter.

'Have you a copy of the letter you sent him?'

'We have.'

'I'm very glad, then,' he said. 'Let's see it here.'

We gave him the letter that had come from the Factor.

'Ah, well,' he said, 'we'll let it be now, and see what he does, then.'

'Well,' I said, 'the Barra people have signed that they won't keep dogs at all. Wilson got them to sign, and they're getting away with the steamer to go home. We'd have to stay two days over here.'

MacDonald turned to me. 'The son of a bitch,' he said. 'But if you take my advice, you'll accept what the Sheriff does to you tomorrow.'

'Indeed we will, and it's likely we'll be right enough.'

The next day, we did that, we went into the court. Black-hearted Wilson arrived, he and MacDonald came in; then the Sheriff came in and went up on to the bench. Wilson began to plead that crofters had no need for dogs; that they might get leave to keep three or four dogs in every township, and that would be sufficient. MacDonald said:

'How will that be sufficient? Will they vote to decide who keeps a dog? If they do, every man will vote to keep a dog himself. Or will they cast lots to see who'll do it? The lot could fall on a bad man and on a bad dog. I've tried that already, and I haven't been able to put it right yet.'

The Sheriff just listened to him. Then the Sheriff took hold of a book and looked at it. Then he read out the Act that had been passed, and the date on which it had been passed; it said that every crofter could keep a dog exempt from licence duty, and every farmer.

Wilson arose against him then, and said:

'Do you call a crofter a farmer?'

'I do,' said the Sheriff, 'if he has a cow and more than one sheep, and works the land where they are, that's a farmer,' he said. 'It appears that everyone who keeps stock, will get to keep a dog like that.' He looked at the book, and said:

'Well, it says in the Act that anyone who has live stock, may keep a dog with exemption from licence duty,' said the Sheriff, turning to him.

'Well,' said Wilson, 'there are plenty who are keeping dogs who've got no land on lease at all.'

'Oh, if they've got livestock,' said the Sheriff, 'they must be keeping it somewhere.'

The Factor then brought him the book in which was the name of everyone in South Uist who had a croft. The Sheriff's clerk brought him the name of everyone who had taken out a dog licence, and read them out. Whenever he came to a man who had no land, the Factor called out that that man had no lease. Then he was put on oath immediately, and questioned by the Sheriff. Did he have stock? Did he have sheep? Did he have cattle?

MacAlpish asked, 'Has he a pig?' Things went on like that. My word, Wilson didn't stop after that; he was determined to win the case. The Sheriff turned to him then, and said:

'Well, Mr Thomas Wilson can interpret the Act as he likes,[11] but we'll manage to make Mr Wilson sit down by means of the Act.' Then he read out the Act to them again, but did Wilson sit down after that! The Sheriff got pretty cross then. He lifted his hand and said:

'Well, you can go on preaching as long as you like, but you won't go any farther than that,' he said, striking the book with his hand. He couldn't get Wilson to keep quiet! He was as good as himself.

Well, we got off clear, except there was a rule that you had to keep a collar on your dog, with your name on the collar, so that if he did any harm, and was caught, it would be known whom he belonged to. That was all right!

After the Land Bill was passed,[12] we got some hill ground for sheep. I was then working on the land more than on the fishing; I was fishing every summer and working on the land the rest of the year. When my father died, I was alone with my mother, and I kept on with the croft; we kept sheep and were doing well enough. After my mother's death, I kept on alone for a year or two, but I wasn't keeping my health very well, and I had to part with my stock, except my sheep, and it was then that I retired and came to live at Frobost. And there you have something of the story of how I spent my life.

NOTES

INTRODUCTION

[1] See *Stories from South Uist*, told by Angus MacLellan, translated from the Gaelic by John Lorne Campbell (Routledge & Kegan Paul, 1961).

[2] The eighteenth-century evangelical Gaelic poet Dugald Buchanan wrote an autobiography in Gaelic, but it is mainly concerned with his spiritual development.

[3] See Minutes of Evidence of the Crofters' Commission.

[4] Tirinie, Borenich, Dalmally are pronounced with the stress on the second syllable; Rowardennan is stressed on the last syllable but one.

1. BOYHOOD ON SOUTH UIST

[1] This sentence in English in the original.

[2] Some of them could speak Gaelic, said Angus, but goodness knows who could understand their Gaelic!

[3] The two paragraphs within brackets were added by Aonghus Beag's sister Mrs Campbell (Bean Nill) at the time the recording was made.

[4] Ranald MacDonald was the chief factor of Lady Gordon Cathcart's Hebridean estates. He gave evidence to the Crofters' Commission in 1883 opposing the crofters' claim for more land and lower rents.

[5] The people who lived on the west side of Uist could grow barley on the sandy 'machair', the people who lived on the east side had peaty soil where oats was the only possible grain crop.

[6] Hoggs are young sheep from weaning-time (which is in August) until the autumn of the next year, usually females kept for breeding. The shearing of such sheep is never done now until the second summer of their life, when they are thirteen or fourteen months old. Conditions must have been very hard if Angus Beag's father had to shear them at their weaning-time to get the wool.

[7] About twelve miles.

[8] The flat sandy plain along the Atlantic coast of Uist. There are always many animals grazing on it. The main road runs down the centre of the island, with side-tracks running off to the farms and villages such as Gearrabhailteas, Bornish, and Loch Eynort.

[9] Astaigh as a' bheinn, i.e. coming over the hilly country round

Loch Eynort to the flat western part of Uist. The shepherd suspected her of having collected tufts of wool off brambles, etc.—indication of the miserly spirit then prevailing on some of the big farms in Uist.

¹⁰ The horses were tethered.

¹¹ *Toit*, a medium-sized stack of oat sheaves, larger than an *adag* but smaller than a *cruach*.

¹² Lochmaddy, in North Uist, the administrative centre of the Inverness-shire Outer Islands, where court cases are heard.

¹³ Probably it was for trespass in search of game rather than for the rabbit itself.

2. THE MILITIA

¹ The Second Battalion the Queen's Own Cameron Highlanders.

² Gaelic *clòsaid*, the small room in the middle of a three-roomed thatched house. It can open off either of the main rooms or off the passage inside the front door, as presumably it did in this case.

³ Aonghus Beag imitates the Lewis accent when telling the story.

⁴ Colonel C. I. Fraser of Reelig has drawn my attention to the following cutting in the *Inverness Courier* of 28th June 1889:

'BOSTOCK'S MENAGERIE

After absence, Bostock's (late Wimbwell's) Menagerie returned to Inverness last week, and the collection was visited on Friday and Saturday by a large number of people. A fine specimen of buffalo, possibly the first seen in Inverness, attracted a good deal of attention. The daring feat of feeding the wolves and lions inside their cages, and giving an illustration of a lion hunt, was done with much coolness by *Sargano*, the well-known tamer, who possesses great power over the animals.'

Colonel Fraser points out that the Second Battalion of the Queen's Own Cameron Highlanders (the Militia) had assembled in Inverness on Friday 21st June 1889 for their 27 days' training at Muir of Ord, and that Saturday the 22nd June, a half-day, must therefore have been the day Angus MacLellan and his friends went to see the Menagerie.

⁵ In South Uist.

3. TIRINIE

¹ Scottish farm-servants then engaged by the 'term' of twelve or six months, starting usually at Martinmas. Something must have gone wrong if Angus's brother left before the term was up.

² In Inverness the square is in front of the station.

³ They could have travelled to Oban on the boat that went through the Caledonian Canal, for eight shillings, but it would have meant staying in Inverness overnight.

⁴ Mr Duncan Menzies, Robert Menzies' son, tells me that it was his father's shepherd who engaged Angus, and Donald Smith, at Oban to come to Tirinie, and that Angus started first as an orra-man. His first job was hoeing turnips.

⁵ Making the long narrow drills in which manure was laid and then closing the earth back over them, either after the planting of the potatoes, or before the sowing of the turnip seed, an operation needing a good deal of skill as the drills had to be absolutely straight and the manure not buried too deep. The work is done with a special kind of plough.

⁶ Literally 'a foot'.

⁷ i.e. turn the earth so that there is a weak hollow at the top of the drill (for the turnip seed to be sown in) don't turn one furrow over the top of the other.

⁸ Bha mi dol mar pheilear mo bheatha ris.

⁹ Actually Glen Golandie.

¹⁰ The work involved here was lifting the turnips, cutting off foliage and roots with a sickle, and leaving the turnips in a tidy line ready to be put into carts and carted to the steading.

¹¹ This would be because Angus's island Gaelic had a bigger vocabulary and many expressions unfamiliar to people in East Perthshire.

¹² These stones have been removed by a subsequent owner, so Miss Mary MacIntosh informs me.

¹³ Miss Mary MacIntosh informs me that Dull was one of the oldest Celtic churches in Scotland. It was a sanctuary, of which four crosses showed the four corners.

¹⁴ Miss Mary MacIntosh tells me this is quite true. Mrs Angus Cameron, the wife or daughter of a schoolmaster, was the *bann-hiosaiche*, seeress. The river Tay was in flood. They had searched six weeks without finding the body. The brother-in-law drew a plan of the bridge, Mrs Cameron said he was lying there fixed by the feet with his head downstream. The man drowned was Archie Menzies, miller.

¹⁵ Duncan Menzies tells me that Sandy was gamekeeper above Coshieville. He thinks this may have happened but to a friend of Sandy and not to Sir Robert Menzies.

¹⁶ Duncan Menzies, now living at West Oaks, Aberfeldy. The youngest, whom Angus calls Ralf, is Alfred Menzies, also living at

Aberfeldy (1961). Neither of them could recollect this incident. If Duncan Menzies was about fifteen years old at the time, this must have happened near the end of Angus' time at Tirinie.

[17] The girl was not very attractive, so I was told! It was lucky for Angus it was only a leg-pull.

[18] Duncan Menzies, the farmer's eldest son (see page xiii). Angus tells me that although the boss at Tirinie always made his men work hard, he was always ready to allow them a day off for any special reason.

[19] Raoide.

4. BORENICH

[1] i.e. for six months.

[2] In English in the original.

[3] chuir e dheth a h-uile stiall mhàthar a bh'air.

5. ROWARDENNAN

[1] Ten o'clock was then closing time.

[2] Literally 'magpie"

[3] Perch. *Perca fluviatilis.*

[4] Bream. *Abramis brama.*

[5] *Coregonus clupeoides.* What Angus MacLellan says about the taste completely contradicts Travis Jenkins's remark that 'they are said to be a delicious article of food, and so much esteemed locally, that they are rarely sent to distant markets'. (*The Fishes of the British Isles,* p. 243).

[6] The Duke of Montrose.

[7] For an account of monstrous eels in Loch Etive, see MacFarlane's Geographical Collections, ii, 148.

[8] Stuadh marbh.

[9] Spriolag.

[10] These words in English in the original.

[11] To make her draw less water and be easier to pull up on to the beach.

[12] Johnny MacIntyre is still living (1961).

[13] Their fathers would have lost their jobs if it had been discovered that they were poaching, as Angus suspected they might be. That was why he was so angry with Blair for telling Kane poaching was going on; he was afraid his friends might get caught and their parents suffer for it.

[14] The watch for the poachers, which Blair had suggested and Angus had sabotaged. (See preceding chapter.)

[15] Leum an nàdar orm.

[16] Bha mi dìreach a' dol a chur cabar air.

[17] i.e. at Rowardennan.

[18] So as to dry the hay in them thoroughly before putting it up in larger stacks.

[19] Last six words in English in the original.

[20] These sentences in English in the original.

[21] These words in English in the original.

[22] These eight in English in the original.

[23] This conversation entirely in English in the original.

[24] This conversation in English in the original.

[25] In English in the original.

[26] These eight words in English in the original.

[27] This sentence in English.

[28] Apparently the term used for the four and six a bottle whisky.

[29] This sentence in English in the original.

[30] agus car ann.

[31] taigh giuthais.

[32] In English in the original.

[33] straointe fosgailte.

[34] tustar.

[35] dìosganaich.

[36] bha a h-uile rud a' cur cogadh rium.

[37] nach ann ort tha 'n oak.

[38] This sentence in English in the original.

[39] i.e. in the half-year.

[40] i.e. he would get fourteen pounds instead of sixteen pounds for the six months from 28th November to 28th May.

[41] i.e. a chance of getting tips.

[42] i.e. the unmarried farm-servants had to live in bothies and make their own meals, getting oatmeal and milk as part of their wages.

[43] Which fixes the year definitely as 1897.

[44] Literally 'the lowest page in his book'.

6. DALMALLY

[1] i.e. to bring potatoes home from the clamp.

[2] 'An rud nach binn leam, cha chluinn mi.' (A proverb.)

[3] Last ten words in English in original.

[4] In English in original.

[5] This conversation in English in the original.

[6] The farm stable was some way away from the hotel, down where the cattle market stance now is.

[7] Nach b'è tu am fear-dùthchadh, i.e. you should know better than to expect that of me, coming as you do from the same place.

[8] In English the original.

[9] i.e. left over for them after the advances they had drawn.

[10] i.e. for the six-months' term.

7. SOUTH UIST AGAIN

[1] Cp. Seonaidh Caimbeul's *Òran nan Giomach* (*Òrain Ghàidhlig le Seonaidh Caimbeul*, p. 10).

[2] The Rodha is a channel between Loch Kildonan and the sea.

[3] Where Fr John Mackintosh was then parish priest. He left Bornish to go to Campbeltown in 1902.

[4] The King Otter was said to be invulnerable to gunshots except for a small white spot on its breast, and in old days its skin was much in demand for bullet-proof waistcoats.

[5] Alasdair Mór MacIntyre was a great Gaelic storyteller. Angus learnt many tales from him.

[6] Bun Loch Aoineort i.e. the top of the loch outside the narrows.

[7] Which was broken up into crofts in 1908. Charles MacLean gave up Gearrabhailteas at Whitsuntide 1910.

[8] This was a famous case, locally considered a resounding victory over tyrannous officialdom. Several Gaelic songs about it are still in circulation. It is referred to by J. P. Day in *Public Administration in the Highlands and Islands of Scotland*, p. 201:

'An Act of 1878 permitted the Commissioners of Inland Revenue to exempt sheep-dogs from licence duty, and since 1906 this power has been delegated to the Sheriff. In 1912 the Congested Districts Board and some private owners opposed 1,596 of these applications for exemption in the Hebrides, but the Sheriff only withheld exemption in 142 cases, and the agent for the applicants was allowed costs in the other cases. He claimed these at £5 10: in each case the sheriff-clerk also claiming his fee of 2/6, altogether a bill of some £7600. The regulations under the Common Grazings Acts now prohibit persons unauthorized by the committee from taking dogs on the common grazings except on the days fixed by them for gatherings.'

[9] 'Board of Agriculture' in the original.

[10] The sea fords between Benbecula and North and South Uist.

[11] This seems to be the intention of the Gaelic, which means literally, 'if it were in the Act that Mr Thomas Wilson mightn't oppose it, or if it was in it that he might'.

[12] In 1911.

GLOSSARY OF AGRICULTURAL TERMS

AIRLES MONEY, a token sum paid by the farmer to the farm-worker to seal a bargain made at a hiring-fair, usually half a crown or a crown.

BEESTINGS, first milk from a cow after calving.

BOTHY, building occupied by unmarried farm-workers, who sometimes did their own cooking.

CHARACTER (p. 153), the reference given to a farm worker on leaving a situation.

CLAMP, a long low pile of potatoes or turnips made in a corner of the field, covered with straw and earth to keep out frost.

DRILLING, the planting of seed on the top of ridges made by a ridging plough.

ELD, barren, not having young.

FACTOR, a bailiff, the representative of the landowner on an estate.

GRIEVE, a farm foreman.

GROUND OFFICER, an estate official under a Factor.

HIRING FAIR, the occasion when farmers and farm-workers entered into agreements for six- or twelve-month engagements. Hiring fairs used to be held in most of the Scottish country towns. The fairs took place a fortnight before the term days, which were on 28th May and 28th November.

HOGG, a year-old sheep.

KEEL, material for making coloured marks on sheep, so as to distinguish age or ownership.

LAND RAID, the forcible occupation of land (usually on a big farm) by landless squatters.

MACHAIR, the sandhills and sandy plain along the Atlantic shore of South Uist, good for grazing and for barley.

MACHINE, a horse-drawn vehicle, a trap.

QUERN, a stone hand-mill, formerly widely used in the Highlands and Islands.

RIDD, an open shed.

SECONDMAN, a second ploughman, man in charge of the second pair of horses on the farm.

SHEILING, a small roughly made building intended for use in the summer only, by persons herding cattle on mountain pastures, or by fishermen fishing lobsters in remote places.

STOB, a fence post.

TERM, the six months' or twelve months' space of time that Scottish farm-workers used to engage with farmers for, see HIRING FAIR.